EDITOR
Samuel C. Stringfield
University of Louisville

FOUNDING CO-EDITOR
John H. Hollifield
Johns Hopkins University

ASSOCIATE EDITORS
Martha Abele Mac Iver, *Johns Hopkins University*
Gina M. Hewes, *Policy Studies Associates*
Wendy G. Winters, *Howard University/CRESPAR*

EDITORIAL BOARD
Lorin Anderson, *University of South Carolina*
James Banks, *University of Washington*
Shelley Billig, *RMC Research Corporation, Denver*
Wade Boykin, *Howard University*
Tony Bryk, *University of Chicago*
Connie Clayton, *Medical College of Pennsylvania*
Amanda Datnow, *University of Southern California*
Alan Davis, *University of Colorado, Denver*
Richard Durán, *University of California, Santa Barbara*
Carolyn Evertson, *Vanderbilt University*
Gerry House, *Institute of Student Achievement*
Faustine C. Jones-Wilson, *Emerita, Howard University*
Glynn Ligon, *Evaluation Software Publishing, Inc.*
Grayson Noley, *University of Oklahoma*
Ellen Pechman, *Policy Studies Associates*
David Reynolds, *University of Exeter*
Steven M. Ross, *University of Memphis*
Robert E. Slavin, *Johns Hopkins University*
Mary E. Yakimowski-Srebnick, *Council of Chief State School Officers*
Robert J. Stevens, *Pennsylvania State University*
Charles Teddlie, *Louisiana State University*
Karen Underwood, *Region No. 14, Comprehensive Center, Tampa*

MANAGING EDITOR
Kirsten Ewart Sundell, *University of Louisville*

ASSISTANT MANAGING EDITOR
Jennifer M. Sawyer, *University of Louisville*

JOURNAL PRODUCTION SUPERVISOR
M.J. Rizzi, *Lawrence Erlbaum Associates, Inc.*

CONTRIBUTOR INFORMATION

Content: The goals of the *Journal of Education for Students Placed At Risk (JESPAR)* are to provide the best research-based information possible to professionals involved with improving the education of students placed at risk and to promote the use of that information through effective communications among researchers, policymakers, and practitioners in the field. *JESPAR* publishes articles geared to academic researchers, policy analysts, and especially to practitioners regarding practical, research-based progress in the field of education for students placed at risk. The journal offers refereed research articles on promising programs; descriptions of promising programs in the field; case studies of "schools that work"; literature reviews; book and report reviews; regular communications on Title I regulations; and school and district practices from federal, state, and local perspectives.

Manuscript Preparation: Prepare manuscripts according to the *Publication Manual of the American Psychological Association* (5th ed., 2001, APA, 750 First Street NE, Washington, DC 20002–4242). Follow "Guidelines to Reduce Bias in Language." Use 1½-in. margins. Type all components double-spaced and in the following order: title page (p. 1), abstract (p. 2), text (including quotes), acknowledgments, references, appendices, footnotes, tables, and figure captions. On the cover page, type article title, author name(s) and affiliation(s), running head (abbreviated title), and name and address of the person to whom requests should be addressed. Research articles should include an abstract of no more than 150 words. Type author notes and acknowledgments at the end of the article (just before the References section). Attach photocopies of all figures. To facilitate anonymous review, only the cover page should include the author's name. Careful effort should be made by the authors to see that the manuscript itself contains no clues to their identities.

Manuscript Submission: Submit four (4) high-quality manuscript printouts to the editor, Sam Stringfield, Journal of Education for Students Placed At Risk, University of Louisville, College of Education and Human Development, Room 333, Louisville, KY 40292. All manuscripts submitted will be acknowledged promptly. Authors should keep a copy of their manuscripts to guard against loss.

Cover Letter: In a cover letter, include the contact author's address and telephone and fax numbers and state that the manuscript includes only original material that has not been previously published and that is not under review for publication elsewhere.

Permissions: Authors are responsible for all statements made in their work and for obtaining permission from copyright owners to reprint or adapt a table or figure or to reprint a quotation of 500 words or more. Authors should write to original author(s) and publisher to request nonexclusive world rights in all languages to use the material in the article and in future editions. Provide copies of all permission and credit lines.

Accepted Manuscripts and Computer Disks: After manuscripts are accepted, authors are asked to (a) submit a disk containing two files (word-processor and ASCII versions of the manuscript); (b) make sure the content of the files exactly matches that of the printed, accepted, finalized manuscript (provide revised printout if necessary); (c) submit camera-ready figures; and (d) sign and return a copyright transfer agreement. It is the responsibility of the contact author to ascertain that all co-authors approve the accepted manuscript and concur with its publication in the journal.

Production Notes: Files of accepted manuscripts are copyedited and typeset into page proofs. Authors read proofs to correct errors and to answer editors' queries. Authors may order reprints of their articles when they receive proofs.

Journal of Education for Students Placed At Risk

SPECIAL ISSUE

Guest Editor's Introduction — 235
    Jeffrey C. Wayman

Linking Data and Learning: The Grow Network Study — 241
    Cornelia Brunner, Chad Fasca, Juliette Heinze, Margaret Honey, Daniel Light, Ellen Mandinach, and Dara Wexler

Using Student-Assessment Results to Improve Instruction: Lessons From a Workshop — 269
    Richard J. Murnane, Nancy S. Sharkey, and Kathryn P. Boudett

Using Data Mining to Identify Actionable Information: Breaking New Ground in Data-Driven Decision Making — 281
    Philip A. Streifer and Jeffrey A. Schumann

Involving Teachers in Data-Driven Decision Making: Using Computer Data Systems to Support Teacher Inquiry and Reflection — 295
    Jeffrey C. Wayman

Identifying and Monitoring Students' Learning Needs With Technology — 309
    Eva Chen, Margaret Heritage, and John Lee

Practices That Support Data Use in Urban High Schools — 333
    Mary Ann Lachat and Stephen Smith

Notes on Contributors — 351

First published 2005 by Lawrence Erlbaum Associates, Inc.

Published 2020 by Routledge
2 Park Square, Milton Park, Abingdon, Oxon OX14 4RN
52 Vanderbilt Avenue, New York, NY 10017

Routledge is an imprint of the Taylor & Francis Group, an informa business

Copyright © 2005 Taylor & Francis.

All rights reserved. No part of this book may be reprinted or reproduced or utilised in any form or by any electronic, mechanical, or other means, now known or hereafter invented, including photocopying and recording, or in any information storage or retrieval system, without permission in writing from the publishers.

Notice:
Product or corporate names may be trademarks or registered trademarks, and are used only for identification and explanation without intent to infringe.

This journal is abstracted or indexed in *Contents Pages in Education; Current Index to Journals in Education; Educational Administration Abstracts; Exceptional Child Education Resources; PsycINFO/Psychological Abstracts; Sage Family Studies Abstracts;* and *EBSCOhost Products.*

ISSN 1082–4669
ISBN 13: 978-0-8058-9434-9 (pbk)

Guest Editor's Introduction

Jeffrey C. Wayman
Center for Social Organization of Schools
Johns Hopkins University

This special issue of the *Journal of Education for Students Placed At Risk* (*JESPAR*) consists of six research articles on the use of student data for educational improvement. The issue had its beginnings in a 2004 American Educational Research Association symposium, "Beyond No Child Left Behind: Using School Data to Improve Student Achievement," in which three of the six articles included in this issue were presented. Noting the quality of the articles and the popularity of the session, *JESPAR*'s editor, Sam Stringfield, pointed out to me that these articles could form the core of an excellent and timely special issue, and that as organizer of the symposium, I was a natural choice to guest edit it. Sam and I have been frequent collaborators on data-use research over the last 3 years, and I consider this issue to be among our best products.

Turning data into information has long been a staple in fields such as business and medicine, but the use of student data for educational improvement has not been widespread. Until only recently, examining student data was a difficult chore for most educators: Data were difficult to access and manipulate, and most educators were unprepared to generate information from data. Further, there were no sanctioned incentives for participating in data use. Consequently, data use was relegated to a few educators with unusual motivation and skills.

This situation is rapidly changing in education. The amount of attention given to student data has recently vastly increased, spurred largely by the No Child Left Behind (NCLB) legislation. As most readers will undoubtedly be aware, NCLB mandates the aggregation and reporting of student achievement data, a task which for most schools represents a drastic change in the way they view and handle student data. Many states were already implementing accountability policies, but NCLB has raised the bar by requiring extensive testing and setting ambitious ob-

---

Requests for reprints should be sent to Jeff Wayman, Center for Social Organization of Schools, Johns Hopkins University, 3003 N. Charles Street, Suite 200, Baltimore, MD 21218. E-mail: jwayman@csos.jhu.edu

jectives for rapid increases in student achievement. Moreover, test scores must be disaggregated by various student subgroups like ethnicity and socioeconomic status.

NCLB is largely responsible for the current attention paid to school data, but data use appears to transcend both politics and faddishness. The power of educational data use does not lie in policy requirements or prescribed testing schedules; rather, it lies in the use of data to produce information in manifold forms. Although NCLB has served to open many eyes to the availability and use of student data, accountability reporting is but one form of data use. The increased attention to data we are currently witnessing has the potential to spawn other thoughtful forms and analyses of data, some of which are already in use, but some of which have yet to be imagined.

Regardless of policy, data use is here to stay. In the abstract, few would argue that creating more information for educators to use is a negative. Perhaps more important is the clichéd notion that data use is an idea whose time has come, given the policy landscape and increased technical capacity to process and deliver data in numerous forms. Educators have made decisions for years armed only with professional judgment, but varied, appropriate forms of student data can now provide educators with an unprecedented amount of information to better understand and diagnose the needs of their students. The applications for data are many. For instance, student data can provide educators with evaluations of teaching methods and policies to better improve educational systems and classroom practice. Student data can provide educators with common ground from which to engage in rich professional conversations and collaborations. Perhaps most important, student data provide a different set of information to augment professional judgment.

Certainly, unlocking an untapped source of knowledge and techniques is exciting to any educator. However, educators are finding the use of data to be a complicated task that reveals a sometimes daunting fact: There is much yet to be learned about best practices for turning data into information. Research questions yet to be answered include, but are not limited to:

- How does a data initiative fit into the larger reform efforts of a school system?
- How can systems be constructed so that information flows freely and efficiently?
- What data practices will school systems, administrators, and teachers find most useful?
- What administrative practices will be most effective in creating a climate of data-driven decision making at the school and classroom levels?
- How can data be delivered to teachers for efficient inquiry into classroom practice?
- What forms of professional development are most helpful to educators?

- What computer technologies are most useful to educators?
- How may teacher and administrator preparation programs proceed at the university level to better prepare educators for information-based inquiry?
- What forms of assessment will prove most informative for different levels of educational systems?
- How do test validity issues affect the quality and utility of information?
- What statistical methods will prove useful for uncovering information at different systemic levels?
- To what degree do various implementations of a data initiative affect educational practice and, ultimately, student outcomes?

Given the nearly limitless questions that exist, it is obvious there is much opportunity for study in the area of school data use. Because data use is relatively new to education, the existing research base lacks rigor, and many oft-cited references are short studies or opinion pieces. The available research is sound but is characteristic of the early stages of a field of study. Thus, it is important to expand and improve the current research base. This need is urgent because school personnel need data and actionable information to meet assessment and accountability standards now. External pressures dictate that schools involve themselves in data use, so the research community needs to provide practitioners, schools, and districts with sound studies of what data-use practices work in schools. Such studies should benefit both researchers and practitioners.

This special issue represents a sizeable step toward this goal. It offers six articles from leading researchers in the area of data use for school improvement. These articles consider the employment of data in improving schools from distinct but overlapping viewpoints, addressing many of the questions listed above. Almost all of the studies consider informed inquiry at the individual educator level, involving teachers and principals. Technology is a constant theme throughout these studies; each research context includes the use of computers to provide efficient access to data. As a group, these articles provide new insight into the use of data to improve schools in a variety of contexts.

The first article, "Linking Data and Learning: The Grow Network Study," comes from work undertaken at the Center for Children and Technology at the Education Development Center in New York City. Born from a larger study examining the use of data in New York City to inform educational decisions, Cornelia Brunner, Chad Fasca, Juliette Heinze, Margaret Honey, Daniel Light, Ellen Mandinach, and Dara Wexler examine the use of data reports from The Grow Network to provide assessment results to teachers and administrators. The Grow Network has a strong reputation for offering well-organized and easily understood reports that help demystify an often overwhelming profusion of formal assessment results. In examining interview data from teachers and administrators, the authors provide detailed descriptions and concrete examples of how the use of these reports affected educational practice; they also describe the limitations inherent in any data-use initiative.

Another recurring theme throughout this issue is the idea that educators are often underprepared to make use of the vast amounts of data now available to them. The issue of professional development is the focus of our second article, "Using Student Assessment Results to Improve Instruction: Lessons From a Workshop," from Richard J. Murnane, Nancy S. Sharkey, and Kathryn P. Boudett at Harvard University. Recently, Dr. Murnane took a 1-year leave of absence from Harvard to work with the Boston public school (BPS) system on assessment issues; various research projects have grown from this relationship. One is the topic of this article, in which the authors describe their experiences conducting a yearlong workshop for BPS educators. This workshop was designed to help educators successfully use assessment data to solve school problems. The importance of committed leadership and the need for structures that enable positive but frank conversations about potentially threatening topics are two important lessons learned from this workshop. Murnane and his colleagues continue to offer this workshop, now rebuilt using knowledge gleaned from the results described in this article.

Although trends, means, and other simple data summaries typically provide the most information needed to inform practice at the school or classroom levels, it is often necessary to engage in complicated analyses at higher levels of the educational system. In the third article, Philip A. Streifer of the University of Connecticut and Jeffrey A. Schumann, principal of Martin Kellogg Middle School in Newington, Connecticut, describe a form of statistical analysis rarely applied to educational data: data mining. Data mining is an exploratory technique that may help the analyst uncover important relationships obscured by traditional statistical approaches. Streifer and Schumann present the results of a preliminary data-mining analysis that used all measures available from a district data warehouse to predict seventh-grade achievement scores. Their models produce impressively high correlations compared to those of other studies, suggesting that data mining may be a promising technique to apply to educational problems. The authors discuss future directions for research using this method.

The fourth article, which I wrote, provides a discussion of teacher use of user-friendly computer data tools. Although NCLB policy creates a large amount of student data, many schools are struggling with NCLB accountability and reporting mandates because school data are often stored in forms that are difficult to access, manage, and interpret. Beyond these struggles, many fear that the lack of provisions for classroom use of these data will discourage teachers from engaging in the potentially rich use of student data for classroom decisions. Fortunately, there are newly available computer technologies that facilitate efficient data access and offer user-friendly access to individuals of all levels of computer expertise. In this article, I describe the availability and features of these computer systems and, perhaps more important, the conditions in which these systems may be used by teachers to inform classroom practice.

In the article that follows, Eva Chen, Margaret Heritage, and John Lee of the National Center for Research on Evaluation, Standards, and Student Testing (CRESST) at the University of California, Los Angeles (UCLA) provide valuable insight into educator use of one of these computer tools, the Quality School Portfolio (QSP), which was developed at CRESST. In evaluating the use of QSP, the authors found that it was used extensively by a variety of educators; they also found that the tool helped facilitate a variety of sound educational practices, notably faculty collaboration and shared planning. Educators in this study did not require extensive training in the use of QSP; most used it to quickly become aware of the utility of data as an evaluative tool. The authors found QSP to be a particularly effective tool for educators to use when diagnosing the needs of at-risk students.

The final article, by Mary Ann Lachat and Stephen Smith of the Center for Resource Management, is titled "Practices That Support Data Use in Urban High Schools." Like Chen and her colleagues, Lachat and Smith undertook an evaluation of a data initiative, this one in five urban schools. This article provides evidence regarding data use in urban schools and identifies facilitators and barriers to data use, varied uses of data for educational improvement, and the policy implications of data use within an urban reform context. The five schools in this study accessed data using the commercially available Socrates Data System. The study provides a valuable analysis of the effects of technology on a data initiative.

I am impressed with the information contained in this volume and excited about the increasing use of student data in improving educational practice in districts, schools, and classrooms. In conversations and presentations regarding data use, I'm often confronted with the viewpoint that technical barriers make data a useful tool only for wealthy schools. On the contrary, I argue that data can be an effective tool for all schools, particularly those in impoverished or underperforming contexts, because of the efficiency of practice that data-use initiatives promise to create. The articles in this volume support that argument. Granted, the price tag for data training and technology may require a substantial initial investment on the part of many districts, but the evidence is mounting that this can also be a cost-effective investment. In the final analysis, any strategy that provides a better quality education to our students is a positive one; data use has particular promise.

Linking Data and Learning: The Grow Network Study

Cornelia Brunner, Chad Fasca, Juliette Heinze,
Margaret Honey, Daniel Light, Ellen Mandinach,
and Dara Wexler
Education Development Center
Center for Children and Technology

> During the last decade, standards, assessments, and accountability have emerged as three prongs of a national education reform movement that has asked district and school administrators to think very differently about educational decision making and the use of data. However, research about data-driven decision making is limited, especially concerning teachers. This article describes findings from a 2-year exploratory study that examined how educators within the New York City public school system are using data—made available to teachers through the print- and Web-based reporting systems of the Grow Network—to inform decisions about teaching and learning. In this article, we summarize what we learned about the specific ways in which teachers and administrators make use of the Grow Reports® to inform educational practices.

In the wake of the No Child Left Behind (NCLB) legislation, increasing attention is being given to accountability and data-driven decision making in public and professional arenas. Although urban districts have faced intense external scrutiny for some time (Fullan, 2000), the shift in funding and the regulatory requirements occasioned by NCLB are prompting educators to think differently about the potential of data to inform instruction and decision making aimed at improving school achievement. School personnel are working hard to develop strategies that support the cohesive use of data across different levels of a school system, and the exploration of how data can inform educational decision making is becoming a main topic of educational policy (Salpeter, 2004; Secada, 2001). Currently, however, research

---

Requests for reprints should be sent to Chad Fasca, Center Editor, EDC's Center for Children and Technology, 96 Morton Street, 7th Fl., New York, NY 10014. E-mail: cfasca@edc.org

about data-driven decision making is limited. Researchers have only a cursory understanding of educators' existing practices, and they know little about how these practices are informed by the influx of data-driven tools.

With funding from the Carnegie Corporation, in the spring of 2002, Education Development Center's (EDC) Center for Children and Technology (CCT) began a 2-year exploratory research study to examine how educators within the New York City public school system are using data to inform decisions about teaching and learning. The opportunity that occasioned this research was a decision by New York City's Board of Education to establish a 5-year contract with an assessment reporting company, the Grow Network,[1] whose mission is to "transform assessment results into instructional tools for teachers, principals, and parents" (Grow Network, 2004) using a mix of print- and Web-based reporting systems. The print materials, called Grow Reports®, deliver customized print reports to teachers, principals, and parents. Grow Reports® for teachers give a concise, balanced overview of standards-based, classwide priorities; group students in accordance with their learning needs; and enable teachers to focus on the strengths and weaknesses of individual students. The reports for principals provide an overview of the school, presenting grade-, class-, and student-level data. The reports for parents provide easy-to-interpret information that explains the goals of the test, their child's performance, and ways in which they can help. The reports for the Web provide teachers with much more detailed information about their students; they also make available links to "teaching tools" that help explain the standards and are solidly grounded in cognitive research about effective math and literacy learning, thereby providing data and instructional tools through the same reporting system.

New York contracted with the Grow Network to provide reports on Grade 3 through Grade 8 English/language arts (ELA) and math assessments for a district serving 30,000 teachers; 5,000 district and school instructional leaders; and 1,200 schools serving approximately 500,000 students. This represented an unprecedented effort to use city-mandated assessment data, coupled with supporting teaching resources and professional development, to improve the quality of educational decision making across multiple levels of the school system.

IMPORTANCE OF THIS STUDY

During the last decade, standards, assessments, and accountability have emerged as the three prongs of the national education reform movement and are now broadly embraced by the education policy community. Over 2 decades ago, with the release of *A Nation at Risk* (National Commission on Excellence in Education,

---

[1]See http://info.grow.net.

1983), the need for higher academic standards became a national issue. Following on the heels of this report, governors, business leaders, and education policymakers gathered at three National Education Summits, in 1989, 1996, and 1999, to create a bipartisan agenda in support of instructional standards and learning environments that promote high expectations for all students.

The NCLB legislation marked the culmination of the move toward increasing accountability and the delineation of achievement standards for all students. The attention that NCLB has brought to educational accountability has been unprecedented; NCLB's presence has been felt in everything from professional educational publications to national and local public media. NCLB holds districts, individual schools, and teachers accountable for student performance—a standard that implies that decision makers (a) have access to data at the appropriate level of aggregation (district, school, teacher, individual student) and (b) are able to interpret them. NCLB requires that disaggregated data be examined for subgroup performance and that all subgroups meet mandated Adequate Yearly Progress (AYP) standards.

Although there is little doubt that accountability measures have risen in popularity among both politicians and the public, the debate about the efficacy of standardized measures of achievement and "high-stakes" testing continues to loom large in education circles (Elliot, 1993; Herman & Golan, 1990; Lemann, 1999; Meyers & O'Connell, 2000; Newman, King, & Rigdon, 1997; Pellegrino, Chudowsky, & Glaser, 2001; Sacks, 1999; Stiggins, 2002; Viadero, 2000). Under NCLB, many traditionally defined high-achieving schools are indeed failing to meet AYP (Robelen, 2003). The consequences are real and significant for educational decision makers and stakeholders, and the pressures on practitioners to improve student performance are increasing (Linn, 1998, 2001a, 2001b, 2003a, 2003b).

One potentially positive consequence of the standards and accountability movement is that district and school administrators are being asked to think very differently about educational decision making and are beginning to use data to inform everything from resource allocation to instructional practice. As researchers at the University of California, Los Angeles (UCLA) Center for Research on Evaluation, Standards, and Student Testing (CRESST) noted:

> Data-based decision-making and use of data for continuous improvement are the operating concepts of the day. School leaders are expected to chart the effectiveness of their strategies and use complex and often conflicting state, district, and local assessments to monitor and assure progress. These new expectations that schools monitor their efforts to enable all students to achieve assume that school leaders and teachers are ready and able to use data to understand where students are academically and why, and to establish improvement plans that are targeted, responsive, and flexible. (Mitchell, Lee, & Herman, 2000, p. 22)

Schools and districts grappling with accountability strategies at the local level are the first to acknowledge that this is a time-consuming process that requires extensive, ongoing professional development work with teachers and school leaders (Council for Basic Education, 2000). It is not surprising, then, that a Council for Basic Education report (2000) concluded: "States and districts will need to think about moving from the three-legged strategy of standards, assessments, and accountability to a model that has a fourth leg—support" (p. 9). As pressures for accountability continue to increase, effective alignment across multiple levels of the school system will become more important in the use of data (Elmore & Abelmann, 1999; Fullan, 2001).

There is no question that data-driven decision making is a complex undertaking, even for the trained educator who understands statistical concepts. As Secada (2001) noted, data should be used to inform decisions, not replace them, and this process requires time and effort. However, researchers lack a sufficient knowledge base to understand the kinds of data-driven practices and strategies that teachers and administrators can use to improve student performance (Pellegrino et al., 2001). Although efforts that focus on helping principals and teachers improve their schools have grown dramatically over the last several decades (Kearns & Harvey, 2000), it is rare to find school communities in which teachers and administrators routinely engage in thinking critically about the relationship between instructional practices and student outcomes. Researchers are equally hard pressed to find substantial numbers of educators who have adequate training and knowledge and are prepared to make appropriate use of data and transform it into useable information and practice (Cizek, 2001; Herman & Gribbons, 2001).

Complexity in the data-driven decision-making process also stems from the systemic structure of school districts. Schools are multilevel organizations composed of dynamically interacting components (Cromey, 2001; Mandinach & Cline, 1994; Senge, Cambron-McCabe, Lucas, Smith, & Kleiner, 2000). The systemic perspective recognizes that because of the cross-level interactions within school systems, data, information, and decision making affect many components of the system simultaneously (Fuqua, Newman, & Dickman, 1999). Thus, the need to consider the issue of how data and information flow through a learning organization such as a school district is critical.

Although a number of technical advancements enabling innovative reporting mechanisms have made data-supported decision making a much more realistic undertaking (Wayman, Stringfield, & Yakimowski, 2004),[2] questions about how educators who are working at different levels of the school system use data to inform decision making remain largely unanswered. Preliminary work on the experiences

---

[2]The Johns Hopkins University Center for Research on the Education of Students Placed at Risk (CRESPAR) maintains a Web site that contains updated information and reviews on technology-based, data-driven decision-making tools. It can be found at: http://www.csos.jhu.edu/systemics/datause.htm

of different data systems is underway at a handful of sites around the country. These include research on the Quality School Portfolio (QSP) developed at CRESST (Mitchell & Lee, 1998); the IBM Reinventing Education data project in Broward County, Florida (Spielvogel et al., 2001), the Texas Education Agency, and the South Carolina Department of Education (Spielvogel & Pasnik, 1999). Research on the role of data systems and applications in practice is also being done in Minneapolis (Heistad & Spicuzza, 2003) and Boston (Sharkey & Murnane, 2003), and on the implementation of QSP in Milwaukee (Thorn, 2002; Webb, 2002). Nonetheless, the New York City school system's partnership with the Grow Network is possibly the largest project of its kind. The study we report on here investigated how data is used and thought about in the classrooms and schools of our nation's largest school district, and thus speaks to important policy concerns about the role of standardized testing and data-driven decision making in education in general.

THE DESIGN OF THE GROW REPORTS®

The Grow Reports® provide an interface to the state and city testing results by organizing raw data into information that is aligned with New York State standards.

For example, a sixth-grade math teacher teaching during the 2003–2004 school year would have access to a customized report that is grouped according to three questions: (a) How did my students do? (b) What do they need to learn? and (c) What tools are on the Web? This report performs a summary and analysis of the data and identifies "class priorities." In response to the first question, the teacher would see the overall scores for all of her sixth-grade students grouped according to the New York State standards across four levels, ranging from Level 1 (*far below standards*) to Level 4 (*far above standards*), along with the students' scale scores. On the second question, the teacher would see how her students did in each standard on the Grade 5 test according to New York State's key ideas. She would also see her students compared as a group to all New York City students. In addition, she would have an overview of class priorities, based on last year's test results on the subskills. The priorities are divided into three levels—need help with fundamentals, need additional instruction, and likely to benefit from advanced work. These levels are calculated by the Grow Network through a complex algorithm comparing each student's subskill results to the performance profile of all Level 4 students on that skill, and so on, for each level.

In addition to the paper-based reports, the Grow Network Web site supports teachers' analysis of the information and instructional decision making with two additional features. The online tools contain instructional materials that define each skill or standard and explain challenges for students in mastering this skill. The class priorities are also linked to resources for teachers and administrators that suggest activities and teaching strategies to promote standards-based learning in the classroom. "Flexible Groupings" of students, which group students by performance in each standard into three categories of performance, are also provided. Finally, the reports also link to external resources approved by the New York City Department of Education.

The design underlying the Grow Reports® encourages differentiated uses of the data it represents. The reports acknowledge that users at different levels in the school system need different kinds of information, different cuts through and across data, and different levels of focus. In this respect, the reports translate raw data into information for different audiences. The teacher version focuses on students who are at various skill levels, so their instructional needs can be addressed. The parent version reports on individual students and their strengths and weaknesses. The administrator version examines larger units, including whole classes, grades, and schools. The reports recognize, in other words, that data mean different things to people in different roles, that the process of turning data into information is different for parents, students, teachers, and administrators because the kinds of decisions they make are different. Different kinds of information are thus useful to each stakeholder. In important respects then, the Grow Reports® represent an ideal way to (a) understand how interpretations vary depending upon one's position in the school system, and (b) investigate how the information that the reports present can serve as a bridge between assessment and instruction. (See Appendix A for sample Grow Reports®.)

RESEARCH DESIGN

To understand how Grow was used across multiple levels of the school system—from teachers, to principals, to district administrators—we used a mix of qualitative and quantitative methodologies and structured the research into three phases. Phase 1 focused on understanding the ways in which central office personnel, along with district superintendents and their education teams, thought about using data to inform decision making. During Phase 1, we conducted structured interviews with 47 educational leaders, including central office stakeholders, superintendents, deputy superintendents, math coordinators, ELA coordinators, staff developers, district liaisons, technology coordinators, directors of research and curriculum, and individuals who work with the United Federation of Teachers. We also spoke with several people representing nongovernmental organizations who are working closely with the New York City schools on issues such as educational reform and professional development.

During Phase 2, we carried out ethnographic research in 15 schools across four school districts in New York City that represented various neighborhoods, student populations, and overall performance levels. Each district identified 4 schools in which we conducted 45 semistructured and open-ended interviews with principals, assistant principals, staff developers, and teachers. In addition, we observed 10 gradewide meetings and/or professional development workshops. To further explore the ways in which teachers think about using assessment information, we also designed a structured interview protocol, using sample Grow Reports® as its basis. We conducted 31 projective interviews with teachers in the two "high-stakes" testing grades—Grades 4 and 8—in New York City, as well as with a sample of sixth-grade teachers. The sample of the upper grade teachers was equally divided between those who teach math and those who teach language arts. Phase 2 of the research helped us to develop a deeper understanding of how classroom teachers think about using data in relation to their everyday practices.

Phase 3 of the study involved the development and administration of two separate surveys across the New York City public school system—one for teachers and one for administrators—and further explored the hypotheses we developed in the previous two phases of work. The surveys asked teachers and administrators about how they interpret data and conceptualize the use of the Grow Reports® for instructional planning. We also inquired about the types of supports needed to fully leverage the use of data to improve instruction.

We disseminated more than 750 surveys to 17 schools across the city and sent an online survey to more than 1,400 teachers and administrators. We received 146 administrator responses and 213 teacher responses from 8 schools.[3] With respect to the teacher responses, we restricted the database to language arts and mathematics teachers who taught students in Grades 4 through 8. Because these are the teachers who use the Grow Reports®, this was done to improve reliability. Furthermore, the restriction of our data to a specific subpopulation of respondents allowed us to triangulate with the qualitative research we conducted, which was also targeted to Grades 4 through 8. The final sample size of reported teacher responses was 96. We compared the experience and education levels of the teachers in our sample to that of New York City teachers as a whole, based on data from the New York City Department of Education's 2001–2002 Annual Report Card (Barr, 2004).[4] See Table 1 for a summary of this information.

The data suggest that despite the limited number of teachers who responded to the survey, they appear to be very similar in terms of education and teaching experience to New York City's overall teaching population. Although by no means a representative sample of the city's teaching population, we have confidence that, with respect to these two demographic variables, they are not a dramatically different group.

---

[3]We attribute the low response rate to a change in administrative priorities in the New York City public schools (see section on *Conducting Research in a Climate of Change*).

[4]The authors would like to thank the Institute for Education and Social Policy at New York University, Steinhardt School of Education, for aid in tracking down this report.

TABLE 1
Comparison of Grow Survey Respondents and New York City Teachers on
Years Teaching and Highest Degree Earned

	Survey Respondents[a] % (n = 96)	NYC Teachers[b] % (n = 947)
Teaching more than 5 years	51	51.4
With a master's degree	71	71.5

[a] $n = 96$. [b] $n = 947$.

CONDUCTING RESEARCH IN A CLIMATE OF CHANGE

It is important to note that, in the course of carrying out this research, the New York City school system underwent a complete reorganization and restructuring. Ultimate control over the school system changed hands from the Board of Education to the mayor. With a new chancellor and deputy at the helm, the newly renamed Department of Education restructured the previous 32 school districts into 10 regions; these are overseen by a regional superintendent and deputy and led by a cadre of local instructional superintendents. Each region encompasses between 100 and 120 schools that now adhere to a uniform curriculum for language arts and mathematics at the elementary level.

Our original intent—to observe how a tool designed to make the data interpretation process more accessible to teachers and administrators impacts decision making at all levels of the New York City school system—had to be altered somewhat during the course of this study. Not only did sweeping administrative and instructional changes take place, but the new leadership also introduced another accountability resource, supplied by The Princeton Review, that provided teachers and administrators with testing results based on assessments administered three times during the current academic year. Although educators still had access to the Grow Reports®, many of the teachers and administrators we spoke to were under the impression that their new priority was to work with The Princeton Review resources.[5] This was a challenging time to observe and chart the movement of an innovation through a system, because the system itself had changed dramatically.

This article draws on a longer, more comprehensive report that can be found on the CCT's Web site,[6] which explores more generally teachers' and administrators' attitudes toward high-stakes testing and the accountability pressures that surround, influence, and inform their work, as well as the kinds of assessment practices in

---

[5] As of the writing of this report, the Grow Reports® are once again being embraced by the current administration and are being used in schools throughout the city.

[6] See http://www.edc.org/CCT

which teachers and administrators routinely engage. In this article, we summarize what we learned about the specific ways in which teachers and administrators make use of the Grow Reports®. The reports proved to be a good focal point for our interviews and surveys. It allowed us to examine both deeply and broadly the actual data produced with this tool and the questions of why such innovations are needed and how to make the best use of them.

EDUCATOR PERSPECTIVES ON THE USE OF GROW REPORTS®

Teachers' Reported Uses of Grow Reports®

During the qualitative phase of the research, we interviewed educators at every level of the New York school system as well as observed gradewide meetings and professional development sessions offered by schools, districts, the Grow Network, and other external organizations. We spent a considerable amount of time talking with classroom teachers about their use of data in classroom decision making and, more specifically, their use of the Grow Reports®. Later, we developed a survey—based on much of what we learned through these conversations and observations—to help validate our findings with a larger sample. In this section, we report on what the teachers and administrators told us about how they use the Grow Reports® in their schools and classrooms.

Throughout the survey and in the interviews, teachers across New York City reported using the Grow Reports® in various ways to meet their classes' and diverse students' academic needs. Grow-using teachers discussed making decisions within the context of certain areas of their instructional practice. We grouped those areas of instructional practice into the following four categories: (a) meeting the needs of diverse learners, with decisions about class priorities, yearlong pacing calendars, weekly lesson plans, grouping, creating Individualized Education Plans (IEPs), and giving individualized assignments and materials appropriate to the students' levels; (b) supporting conversations with parents, students, fellow teachers, and administrators about students' learning; (c) shaping teachers' professional development by reflecting on their own practice; and (d) encouraging self-directed learning by giving the data to students.

Before exploring more intensely teachers' uses of the Grow Reports®, we want to mention two basic findings about using Grow. First, during the interviews, we learned that teachers found the reports to be clear and comprehensible. All the teachers understood the basic aspects of the reports, such as the students' scores and the New York State performance levels. As a company, the Grow Network was reported to be very responsive to suggestions from the teachers about clarifying and improving the reports.

Second, with respect to frequency of use, we found that 37% of teachers used the Grow Reports® monthly, with 32% of the teachers reporting using the reports three to six times throughout the year.

Meeting the Needs of Diverse Learners

Noting that the Grow Reports® provided them with more information about students than they previously had access to, teachers said that they looked at the data mostly to know "where their students are." In the interviews, teachers commonly understood the test results in relative terms of their students' strengths and weaknesses. The survey results indicate the same pattern, as most respondents (91%) reported using the Grow Reports® to determine classwide strengths and weaknesses. Several teachers noted that they relied on the data more at the beginning of the year when they didn't know their class or students that well. A fifth-grade teacher in the Bronx said, "In the beginning of the year, before I really know the kids well, [Grow] is a good sort of first idea of what I'm dealing with and what their needs are."

Teachers at both the elementary and middle school levels explained that by looking at the Grow Reports®, they could see in which areas their overall class and individual students scored high and on which measures they scored low; these teachers could then alter their instruction accordingly. Many teachers used the information to focus more intensely on, or include more practice in, the areas in which students scored low. For example, one teacher explained that when looking at the reports, she asked herself, "Where is my class lacking?" Once she identified those skills, she searched for ways to thread them throughout her instructional program. Another teacher stated that she didn't rely solely on the Grow data to inform her instruction. "I spiral," she reflected. "If they know something, I will make it a homework assignment to see how much they remember and if I need to review or re-teach. I will spiral topics throughout the whole year."

Conversely, some teachers shifted instruction time away from areas in which students scored well. For example, one 1st-year sixth-grade math teacher in the Bronx said that she liked the Grow Reports® because once she learned in which areas her students had performed well, she didn't have to "teach what they are stronger in." But teachers did not rely solely on the test results. Several teachers said that certain concepts or skills were more difficult for students to master, so they incorporated them into larger units or created focused minilessons for constant reinforcement.

The survey results support what we learned in the interviews and give a larger picture of how widely used the Grow Reports® are for certain types of decisions. On the survey, 89% of Grow users reported using the resource to "set priorities about what they teach." A majority of Grow users also responded that they used the reports to inform decisions when planning lessons (76%) and when deciding on minilessons

(71%). A little more than half of the teachers (51%) reported that they used Grow data when creating yearlong pacing plans.

In addition to using the Grow Reports® for guidance in classroom instruction, many teachers also reported using the reports to meet the needs of individual students, especially those who were struggling. Teachers mentioned strategies such as grouping, creating IEPs, and giving individualized assignments and materials appropriate to students' levels. The survey responses supported these observations, as 89% reported using Grow to differentiate instruction. Teachers reported utilizing several different strategies to differentiate instruction, such as teaching using small leveled groups, assigning differentiated class work or homework corresponding to students' needs, constructing peer-tutoring situations consisting of a low-performing and a high-performing student working together, and/or tutoring students one on one.

One group of learners who often figured prominently in teachers' interviews were the students who had scored just above or below the edge of proficiency (the top of the range for Level 2 or at the bottom of Level 3 in New York's four-level system, in which 1 = failing, 2 = below standard, 3 = at standard, and 4 = above standard). This population was often referred to as the "bubble kids" because of their statistical location in a bubble of scores near the cutoff point. Because the probability of moving these students is much higher, some teachers and administrators reported targeting them for extra resources, such as pull-outs and after-school and special programs, in an effort to move them up a level or ensure they did not slide down a level. The format of the Grow Reports® made identifying these students very easy. A first-year seventh-grade language arts teacher in Harlem said:

> The difference is very important. The 615 [score level] could easily be at the next level. To get the kids' scores to move, it's a discipline issue. If there were less [sic] disruptions in the classroom, the kids who are right at the cutoffs would be able to learn what they need.

Other teachers handled these students differently. A fifth-grade teacher in Harlem said:

> I'd probably put him in the higher group even if he placed below them so he'd be around those kids and give the extra push. So work a little bit above his level because he could probably handle it. A lot of what's done is just for a change of instruction, so in other words, give him what the higher kids are doing.

Even though teachers reported that they could use the Grow data when making decisions about grouping, especially with the "bubble kids," many were careful to note that the Grow data was "one small piece" that they considered in conjunction with other forms of data collected from a wide array of assessments, including observations, in-class assignments, daily quizzes, and unit pre- and posttests, to name a few. Moreover, teachers added that the data on the Grow Reports® had "declining value" as the year progressed, in part because students take the exam roughly 6 months before the reports are distributed. According to a 1st-year seventh-grade math teacher in Harlem, "The more time that goes by before you get it, the less value it has." Elementary school teachers, in particular, noted that their students change so much throughout the year that they must base their decisions about grouping and regrouping on ongoing assessment. "If they progress, you take them out and move them into a different group," said a fifth-grade teacher in the Bronx.

In addition to grouping, teachers reported that providing students with a multitude of materials and manipulatives to create multiple entry points into the content was another way to target instruction on students' strengths and weaknesses. A fourth-grade teacher in Harlem remarked, "We have a number of different materials in different lengths, of different subject matter, so it's cross-content plus curriculum that enables them to have exposure and success in various different activities." Teachers agreed that when selecting or modifying instructional materials or assignments, it was beneficial to know where students were in terms of the standards and skills. Some said they differentiated instruction by giving certain students modified in-class and/or homework assignments that corresponded to their ability levels. Sixty percent of the survey respondents who identified themselves as Grow users said that they used the reports when creating homework assignments. In interviews, some teachers also said they used entirely different textbooks or supplementary materials to work with different students. For example, one teacher used information found in the Grow Reports® to create different math homework calendars, which targeted students' specific strengths and weaknesses.

Supporting Conversations

The Grow Reports® also helped encourage discussions about student learning. Most of the teachers we spoke with talked about using the Grow Reports® in conversations with teachers, parents, administrators, and students. They found the Grow Reports® to be a good starting point for conversations as well as something "concrete" to show parents, administrators, other teachers, or the students themselves when discussing where the class or individual students were in learning and where they needed to go. One sixth-grade teacher in Harlem said:

> I explain the Grow Reports® to the kids and to their parents. I point out where they are weak and encourage them to focus on that skill. Some kids get nervous about it, but kids handle it well. Kids take the initiative and some kids take the textbook home and will do extra problems in areas where they need help. Some parents put the Grow Reports® up on the fridge.

The responses on the survey showed a similar pattern of use. Sixty-two percent of teachers reported using Grow as the basis for conferences with parents, 52% with students, 47% with other teachers, and 38% with administrators and/or staff developers.

Shaping Professional Development

Several teachers said that when analyzing the Grow Reports® and identifying their classes' strengths and weaknesses, they took an opportunity to reflect on their own teaching practice. Seventy-seven percent of the Grow users who completed the survey reported that they used the Grow Reports® to reflect on the effectiveness of their own instruction. Teachers explained that seeing, for example, that the majority of students scored low on a skill, such as cause and effect, would cause them to assess how they taught that specific skill. Some teachers reported that looking at the reports made them realize they weren't even teaching some of the standards and skills on which the students were tested. Furthermore, several new teachers, having taught for 3 years or less, said that they referred to the Grow Reports® to learn more about what to teach. A fourth-grade teacher in Harlem remarked, "[Grow] motivated me to go and research it on my own. I printed out all of the skills for ELA and math. I wanted to know which skills the students needed to know."

Supporting Self-Directed Learning

Another interesting use of Grow that emerged during the fieldwork was the dissemination of the data to students as a way to encourage them to take ownership of their own learning. Because the Grow Network creates a parent report, many teachers spoke about giving Grow Report® to the students to take home to their parents. A small but sizeable group of teachers talked about sharing the reports (or the data from the reports) with their students so that students would be not only aware of their performances on the test but also encouraged to take responsibility in terms of their own academic progress.

Although all of these teachers hoped that sharing individual data with their students would help them take ownership over their own academic performance and learning, the ways by which teachers did this varied. One school created individual binders for each student with the Grow Report® in the front. Some teachers in that school simply distributed the reports to students without structuring any time to discuss them with students. They instructed students to look at and keep them in the front of one of their binders or notebooks. Other teachers dedicated time to discuss the report's structure with their whole class, explaining what scores meant in addition to offering students strategies for improving their scores. Students could not only see their scores but also analyze them, so they would know which skills they needed to improve. Students could then hone in on those standards or skills and take concrete steps to practice and master them.

A handful of teachers actually met with each of their students individually to discuss the scores, identify strengths and weaknesses, set goals, and strategize about how to meet them. One example came from a middle school in Harlem, where an eighth-grade Communication Arts teacher who has been teaching for more than 30 years held individual conferences with each of his eighth-grade students to discuss scores and identify areas or skills that needed improvement. According to the teacher, he used the student's individual Grow Report® as a starting place for these discussions, and as a motivator. Together, he and the student looked at the Grow Report® to identify where the student scored high and low. The student then wrote down on a note card at least three skill items or standards from the report on which he or she wanted to work. The student was instructed to keep the note card. Whenever they had free time during class, students could work on the skills listed on their note cards in CTB/McGraw Hill workbooks, which were stored in the back of his classroom and broken down into chapters aligned with the test. Students could then practice answering test-like questions that specifically addressed the skills with which they were struggling. The teacher shared that this was not only a way for him to incorporate test preparation into his curriculum without letting it overwhelm the curriculum, but also a means for addressing individual students' needs.

Administrators' Reported Uses of the Grow Reports®

New York City district- and building-level administrators reported using the Grow Reports® to gain a greater understanding of the educational and instructional concerns particular to the level of the education system at which they worked. One superintendent explained how administrators used Grow Reports® on both the district and school level. All schools and classrooms received the Grow Reports®. Administrators felt that "data"—including the data that the Grow Network reported on—would drive their decision making toward more informed educational choices for students, teachers, and themselves as administrators. They used this data in many ways, ranging from articulating administrative needs to putting forth an educational vision for their school or the larger school district, paying attention to their school's diverse student needs.

Looking across the interviews and surveys, we found that the administrators' uses for the Grow Reports® could be grouped into four main categories: (a) identifying areas of need and targeting resources, (b) planning, (c) supporting conversations, and (d) shaping professional development activities for teachers. However, depending upon the administrators' position (e.g., superintendent for curriculum, district math coordinator, school principal, or staff developer), they synthesized the data organized by the Grow Reports® and implemented their decisions into the school or district in slightly different ways.

Identifying Areas of Need and Targeting Resources

Administrators explained that the Grow Reports® helped them to identify grade, class, and schoolwide strengths and weaknesses that could then be used to make decisions about planning, shaping professional development activities, and determining student performance and demographics. According to the survey, a large majority of administrators (86%) reported that they "sometimes," "often," or "always" used the Grow Reports® to identify high-performing students.

An even larger majority (93%) said they used the reports to identify low-performing students for additional resources. The administrators spoke quite frequently about the "bubble kids." They felt pressure from their district leaders regarding students on the cusp. For example, a director of math and assessment in a Queens district described her yearly data training for principals: "We had some really powerful conversations—I said it is important to know who the children on the cusp are and what it'll take to move them." A deputy superintendent described a district policy that had been in place for 1 year that he termed "moving test scores": The district identifies students who are near the proficiency level (at the top of Level 2 but just under Level 3) and requires principals to target this small group of students, placing them with the best teachers and extra supports.

Other administrators reported that their district was targeting test-preparation programs toward students with high Level 2 proficiency and low Level 3 proficiency. One school was using Grow to help them target these students for academic intervention services. As a principal in Canarsie commented, "All some students need, by the grace of God, is to pick up one or two more questions." Other schools would ask teachers to identify their "bubble kids," so that the school could offer a "push-in" teacher to cover a specific skill or strategy. A staff developer in Canarsie spoke about pulling students near the cusp from across the fourth-grade classes to prepare them for the test:

> I pulled out the 10 kids from each class that narrowly missed Level 3. I took some 610, 620; I even took some 590 [referring to scaled scores] if I thought that the kid had a solid test [but] just missed it by a question. And I divided them into groups ... and what I do is take similar questions from the GROW report.

One principal in Harlem described how her school used data:

> Okay, we know what resources we have in the school. We have AIS [Academic Intervention Services] teachers—reading and math—our Extended Day program, our Title I funding ... so these are the kids we are going to start identifying who are in need

of remedial work, not that we are going to forget about the others. Nonetheless, we are going to look at these [kids] because they can sway this way or that way, so I say to the teachers, "Who do we feel could be pushed onto Level 3? Who is in jeopardy, at risk of either staying at the status quo or regressing?" We don't want that, so ... what we do is we divvy up these kids, and the AIS teacher then focuses her instructional program on those students. Likewise with the advanced kids, we have Advanced Placement classes in reading and math and so on. Then those teachers already know who they are. Now they don't know that unless they have the data, or we give them that data, or they themselves have access.

Administrators also felt that Grow was helpful at the teacher level in addition to the student level. One superintendent explained, "Grow allows you to combine test results and longitudinal analysis to diagnose a school's strengths. This helps make decisions about professional development and resource allocation." Another superintendent believed that the data could "help new principals to identify good teachers" and "meet one of his challenges by supporting the school leaders."

However, a little more than half of the administrators (54%) who responded to the survey reported that they used the Grow Reports® to "sometimes," "often," or "always" allocate budgetary resources. This data suggests that although administrators commonly talk about using data to determine how to allocate resources, they are less likely to put these ideas into practice.

Planning

Once administrators identified which students, teachers, and resources they needed to target, this information helped them to focus their school or district planning activities. Administrators explained that they used the data on the Grow Reports® to plan for setting school and district priorities and for instructional programs, as a district-level math and science coordinator in Manhattan explained during an interview:

> We get general test data but they don't tell us much. Grow can tell us where the weaknesses are ... I have schools that are at different levels. I have teachers at different levels. Grow helps map out what district facilitators need to target.

One assistant principal in the Bronx explained: "Grow helps me target resources, such as after-school and extended-day programming, to students in need."

According to the survey, the administrators reported using the Grow Reports® for planning activities in a variety of ways. Eighty-three percent of the administrators stated that they used the Grow Reports® "sometimes," "often," or "always" to "set schoolwide priorities." Eighty-four percent said that they "sometimes," "often," or "always" used the Grow Reports® to plan test-preparation activities. Meanwhile, 66% said that they "sometimes," "often," or "always" used the reports to make yearlong pacing calendars.

Although most administrators made use of the Grow Reports®, they did so with lesser frequency than did the teachers. According to the survey, 4% of administrators used the Grow Reports® once a week or more, compared to nearly 7% of teachers; 12% of administrators used it once a month, compared to 19% of teachers. However, 43% of the administrators used the Grow Reports® three to six times a year, compared to 32% of teachers. And although administrators, like teachers, noted that Grow provides useful information, administrators did not look to this data exclusively to make decisions because the report is based only on a single test. As one superintendent said, "You have to take into consideration how valid or current the data [are] when you are using the previous year's data. This is why you have to compare Grow with all of the other data sources."

School-based administrators also believed that Grow should be used along with other forms of data to assist with planning activities, as an assistant principal in Harlem noted:

> Grow is not a sole diagnostic. I see it as one piece. We use it in conferences and goal setting with students, and together with portfolios to create a portrait. It's constant because a student can grow in six weeks. It's wonderful. A fourth-grader can recover and jump ahead. A combination of assessments shows change over time. Grow is static.

A principal in Canarsie echoed this statement: "You must look at the whole picture and never use just one source." In other words, using the Grow Reports® for planning purposes was just one resource in addition to many others that administrators used throughout the school year.

Supporting Conversations

In interviews, many of the administrators spoke about how the Grow Reports® assisted with framing conversations they had with teachers, parents, or other administrators related to student learning, professional development for teachers, or addressing school or district challenges. According to the survey, 87% of administrators reported using the Grow Reports® to conference with teachers, 73% with other administrators or staff developers, 70% with parents, and 55% with students. In addition, about 46% of the administrators also reported using the Grow Reports® to "often or always conference individually or in small groups with teachers."

During the interviews, school-based administrators explained that they used the Grow Reports® and related materials in "gradewide meetings," "to inform minilessons," "to connect reading and writing activities," and "as a way to start a dialogue with teachers to identify which categories the students couldn't answer and develop strategies to respond."

One principal described how she wanted her teachers at an upcoming gradewide literacy meeting to "review their Grow Reports® and to identify a gradewide challenge and then to decide on a few teaching strategies." She explained that she felt it was "important for colleagues to realize that they all have the same type of kids. Teachers tend to always think that 'their kids' are different from other teachers' students." She hoped that this conversation would contribute to teachers sharing strategies and approaches, and that together they would "think through what we need to do" for the school. "Mandating does not work," she said. She hoped that the teachers would make the decisions.

Some administrators also felt that the Grow Reports® were a useful resource for parents. One assistant principal in the Bronx explained that in her school, testing and test scores had been very public and the Grow Reports® were openly shared with students and their parents. "Parents are relieved by it," she said:

> They feel it gives them good feedback and they can see resources, which is important for them to feel like there's something they can do to help their child. If a child is in need, now parents can see it. It breaks it down ... what you can do, what you can make better, and the steps to take to get there.

District administrators also embraced using the Grow data with parents and spoke about using the Grow Reports® to prepare for parent talks. One superintendent explained that to deal with language and literacy challenges in the district, "if parents could use the [Grow] data, this would be a major push."

Shaping Professional Development Activities

The instructional resources incorporated into the Grow Reports® were approved by the New York City Department of Education and aligned to state standards. Because the Grow Reports® were aligned with standards and objectives that the school and district viewed as important, administrators found that the reports were often a good fit for shaping professional development activities.

Many district- and school-based administrators provided professional development workshops for principals and/or for teachers on how to use Grow; however, some administrators took using Grow to another level. As one superintendent explained, "The ultimate goal is for teachers to have flexible grouping in their classroom. Grow provides the easy part of this—then the hard part of this is up to us: how to use it!" Thus, Grow became used both as the focus of a professional development activity (typically in a workshop format) and for shaping other professional development activities, such as helping teachers to create differentiated instructional activities or learning about school- or districtwide standards and goals through their close alignment to the Grow Reports®.

Eighty-two percent of the administrators surveyed said they either "sometimes," "often," or "always" used the Grow Reports® to make professional development decisions. Administrators interviewed said that they found it helpful to check their own assessments against those of the Grow Reports® and to then use both to guide teachers, a process described by one staff developer in the Bronx:

> I use it just as kind of a backup. ... I think to find out myself. Each kid's an individual so I actually like to work with the kid and show the teachers how to work with the children and find out what he needs. And then to double confirm what I think we need to work on, we'll look at the Grow Report. ... That'll kind of be like telling me that I'm on the right track. If I see that there's something different ... we'll go back to the child and we'll see where the inconsistency is.

She used the report to help guide professional development at multiple levels—for herself as an administrator, for the teacher, and for developing differentiated instruction and assessment activities for the student.

CONCLUSION

Data-Driven Decision Making and the Grow Reports®

First and foremost, data-driven decision making requires that appropriate data be turned into useful information that can aid in the making of knowledgeable and informed decisions (Ackoff, 1989; Drucker, 1989). Digital technology has played a major part in enabling educators to interact with appropriate data that they can use to make decisions on a more informed basis. Specifically, the relative ease of use and sophistication of data-gathering, storage, and delivery systems has made data accessible in a meaningful format to whole sets of constituents whose access to data in the past was either nonexistent or presented in dense and unintelligible reports (Wayman et al., 2004). This research focused primarily on how this increased access to data might inform and support decisions about children's education. We were interested in how the Grow Reports® would be used by educators to support decision making at various levels of the system.

As a tool, the Grow Report® tries to underscore the ways in which test data can be used to inform instruction, not just accountability. By design, it provides a format that builds a bridge between standards, testing results, and instructional strategies. It provides educators with guidance on how to cope with students' differential learning patterns and provides teachers with a rationale for differentiating instruction. Our task was to examine how this concerted effort to introduce teachers to data in the context of instructional decision making affected teachers and administrators.

Teachers use the testing data provided in the Grow Reports® to plan activities, lessons, and units. They sometimes use it as a starting point for conversations with students, parents, specialists, and administrators. Some teachers plan their own professional development, based on test data, to focus on areas in which they think their students need more help. But more than anything else, teachers use test data to allocate their own resources: time, attention, practice, and homework.

In contrast to teachers, administrators use the Grow Reports® to help them make building-level decisions, such as allocating resources, targeting those students who are most in need of additional support or who can benefit from more advanced instruction, and starting conversations that help them communicate and establish leadership priorities. In this way, they help to support and focus the priorities of staff developers and instructional leaders. Reports are also used to identify strengths and weaknesses in classrooms and across school buildings so that professional development can be focused on those areas of instruction most in need of improvement.

Although administrators, like teachers, stress the importance of using multiple sources of data when making decisions, they, too, know that raising test scores is the ultimate measure of their success. As a result, administrators in New York encourage teachers to focus on the students who are on the cusp of meeting proficiency on the high-stakes test. In particular, the students who are at the top of Level 2 in New York's four-level system and who can be moved up to Level 3 are the most crucial for accountability. Getting the failing students to where they are doing better—though still below standard—or getting students who are doing well enough to do really well does not count for as much as moving as many of the kids who are at the top of Level 2 to the bottom of Level 3. For teachers and administrators, this means identifying those "bubble" students, making sure they spend enough time practicing the skills they need for the test, pitching instruction to the areas they are having difficulty with, or creating ability groups designed to help students move up a notch.

As a tool that aligns test results with standards and instructional strategies, the Grow Reports® appear to be highly successful in creating a navigational framework for educators. For teachers, the Grow Reports® present data in a meaningful format from which teachers can draw the information they need to support differentiating instruction and thinking about students' weaknesses as well as their strengths. In this sense, the Grow Reports® can be said to be playing a critical role in helping teachers navigate the tensions that exist in a high-stakes climate between the accountability model of schooling, where data from standardized tests drive assessment and practically define the standards, and a reform model, where diversity is considered in the curriculum and defined by differentiated pedagogical practices.

For administrators, the reports represent a means to meet accountability requirements. This is not surprising given that administrators face real penalties. In New

York City, principals can be removed from schools that are not making adequate progress as measured by testing results; superintendents and their deputies can be replaced; and schools and districts can lose resources when students chose to transfer from failing schools to better performing ones. From an accountability standpoint, the "bubble kid" strategy makes sense. The danger of this kind of strategy is that it tends to direct resources to one group of students at the expense of others (Confrey & Makar, 2002). Accountability requires that schools get the averages up, which means focusing more attention on the test and the tested skills some students lack than on expanding and improving the skills of those who are failing or succeeding.

The limitations of the Grow Reports® are, of course, that they rely on a single standardized test. As a result, the way in which they present evidence of differential learning is limited. However, the teachers and administrators with whom we spoke were extremely cognizant of this limitation, and teachers, in particular, found creative ways to use the information contained in Grow to inform both instructional practices and administrative decision making. When teachers in this study talked about data-driven decisions, it was almost invariably in the context of accountability—helping students meet standards as evidenced by their performance on standardized tests. Yet, we also heard teachers discussing data-driven decision making in the context of a reform agenda in which diversity, both cultural and cognitive, is as central to learning as standards are to the accountability perspective.

ACKNOWLEDGMENTS

This research was supported with a grant from the Carnegie Corporation.

REFERENCES

Ackoff, R. L. (1989). From data to wisdom. *Journal of Applied Systems Analysis, 16*, 3–9.
Barr, J. M. (2004). *Teacher location choice and distribution of quality*. Newark, NJ: Rutgers University, Department of Economics.
Brophy, J. (2001). *Teaching*. Brussels, Belgium: International Academy of Education.
Cizek, G. J. (2001). Conjectures on the rise and fall of standards setting: An introduction to context and practice. In G. J. Cizek (Ed.), *Setting performance standards: Concepts, methods, and perspectives* (pp. 3–18). Mahwah, NJ: Lawrence Erlbaum Associates, Inc.
Confrey, J., & Makar, K. (2002). Developing secondary teachers' statistical inquiry through immersion in high-stakes accountability data. In D. Mewborn, P. Sztajn, & D. White (Eds.), *Proceedings of the twenty-fourth annual meeting of the North American Chapter of the International Group for the Psychology of Mathematics Education PME-NA24* (Vol. 3, pp. 1267–1279). Columbus, OH: The ERIC Clearinghouse for Science, Mathematics, & Environmental Education.
Council for Basic Education. (2000). *Closing the gap*. Washington, DC: Author.
Cromey, A. D. (2001, Spring). Data retreats: A conduit for change in schools. *Newsletter of the Comprehensive Center-Region VI, 6*, 21–23.

Drucker, P. F. (1989). *The new realities: In government and politics/in economics and business/in society and world view.* New York: Harper & Row.
Elliot, E. (1993). National testing and assessment strategies: Equity implications of leading proposals for national examinations. In M. T. Nettles (Ed.), *Equity and excellence in educational testing and assessment* (pp. 415–424). Boston: Kluwer Academic.
Elmore, R., & Abelmann, C. (1999). *When accountability knocks, will anyone answer?* Philadelphia: University of Pennsylvania, Center for Policy Research in Education.
Fullan, M. (2000). The three stories of education reform. *Phi Delta Kappan, 81,* 581–584.
Fullan, M. (2001). *The new meaning of educational change* (3rd ed.). New York: Teachers College Press.
Fuqua, D. R., Newman, J. L., & Dickman, M. (1999, Winter). Barriers to effective assessment in organizational consultation. *Consulting Psychology Journal: Practice and Research, 51*(1), 14–23.
Grow Network. (2004). *About the Grow Network.* Retrieved April 1, 2004, from http://grownetwork.com/
Heistad, D., & Spicuzza, R. (2003, April). *Beyond zip code analyses: What good measurement has to offer and how it can enhance the instructional delivery to all students.* Paper presented at the annual meeting of the American Educational Research Association, Chicago, IL.
Herman, J., & Golan, S. (1990). *Effects of standardized testing on teachers and learning.* Los Angeles: University of California, National Center for Research on Evaluation, Standards, and Student Testing.
Herman, J., & Gribbons, B. (2001). *Lessons learned in using data to support school inquiry and continuous improvement: Final report to the Stuart Foundation* (CSE Tech. Rep. No. 535). Los Angeles: University of California, Center for the Study of Evaluation.
Kearns, D. T., & Harvey, J. (2000). *A legacy of learning.* Washington, DC: Brookings Institute.
Lemann, N. (1999). *The big test.* New York: Farrar, Straus & Giroux.
Linn, R. L. (1998). *Standards-based accountability—Ten suggestions* (Policy Brief No. 1). Los Angeles: University of California, National Center for Research on Evaluation, Standards, and Student Testing.
Linn, R. L. (2001a). *The design and evaluation of educational assessment and accountability systems* (CSE Tech. Rep. No. 540). Los Angeles: University of California, National Center for Research on Evaluation, Standards, and Student Testing.
Linn, R. L. (2001b). *Reporting school quality in standards-based accounting systems* (Policy Brief No. 3). Los Angeles: University of California, National Center for Research on Evaluation, Standards, and Student Testing.
Linn, R. L. (2003a). Accountability: Responsibility and reasonable expectations. *Educational Researcher, 32*(7), 3–13.
Linn, R. L. (2003b). *Requirements for measuring adequate yearly progress* (Policy Brief No. 6). Los Angeles: University of California, National Center for Research on Evaluation, Standards, and Student Testing.
Mandinach, E. B., & Cline, H. F. (1994). *Classroom dynamics: Implementing a technology-based learning environment.* Hillsdale, NJ: Lawrence Erlbaum Associates, Inc.
Meyers, E., & O'Connell, F. O. (2000, May 31). The test doesn't tell all. *Education Week, 19,* pp. 34, 37.
Mitchell, D., & Lee, J. (1998, September). *Quality School Portfolio: Reporting on school goals and student achievement.* Paper presented at the National Center for Research on Evaluation, Standards, and Student Testing Conference, Los Angeles, CA.
Mitchell, D., Lee, J., & Herman, J. (2000, October). Computer software systems and using data to support school reform. In the Joyce and Johnston Foundations (Sponsors), *Technology's role in urban school reform: Achieving equity and quality.* Symposium conducted at the Wingspread Meeting of the Education Development Center, Center for Children and Technology, New York.
National Commission on Excellence in Education. (1983). *A nation at risk.* Washington, DC: Author.

Newman, F. W., King, M. B., & Rigdon, M. (1997, Spring). Accountability and school performance: Implications from restructuring schools. *Harvard Educational Review, 67*(1), 41–74.

Pellegrino, J. W., Chudowsky, N., & Glaser, R. (2001). *Knowing what students know: The science and design of educational assessment.* Washington, DC: National Academy Press.

Robelen, E.W. (2003, September 3). State reports on progress vary widely. *Education Week.* Retrieved December 1, 2004, from http://www.edweek.org/ew/articles/2003/09/03/01ayp.h23.html

Sacks, P. (1999). *Standardized minds: The high price of America's testing culture and what we can do to change it.* Cambridge, MA: Perseus Books.

Salpeter, J. (2004). Data: Mining with a mission. *Technology and Learning, 24*(8), 30–37.

Secada, W. (2001, Spring). From the director. *Newsletter of the Comprehensive Center-Region VI, 6,* 1–2.

Senge, P., Cambron-McCabe, N., Lucas, T., Smith, B., & Kleiner, A. (2000). *Schools that learn.* New York: Doubleday.

Sharkey, N., & Murnane, R. (2003, April). *Helping K–12 educators learn from student assessment data.* Paper presented at the annual meeting of the American Educational Research Association, Chicago.

Spielvogel, B., Brunner, C., Pasnik, S., Keane, J. T., Friedman, W., Jeffers, L., John, K., & Hermos, J. (2001). *IBM Reinventing Education Grant Partnership Initiative: Individual site reports.* New York: Education Development Center, Center for Children and Technology.

Spielvogel, B., & Pasnik, S. (1999). *From the school room to the state house: Data warehouse solutions for informed decision-making in education.* New York: Education Development Center, Center for Children and Technology.

Stiggins, R. (2002). Assessment crisis: The absence of assessment for learning. *Phi Delta Kappan, 83,* 758–765.

Thorn, C. (2002). *Data use in the classroom: The challenges of implementing data-based decision-making at the school level.* Madison: University of Wisconsin, Wisconsin Center for Education Research.

Viadero, D. (2000, May 3). High-stakes tests lead debate at researchers' gathering. *Education Week, 19,* 6.

Wayman, J. C., Stringfield, S., & Yakimowski, M. (2004). *Software enabling school improvement through the analysis of student data* (Report No. 67). Baltimore, MD: Johns Hopkins University, Center for Research on the Education of Students Placed At Risk.

Webb, N. (2002, April). *Assessment literacy in a standards-based urban education setting.* Paper presented at the annual meeting of the American Educational Research Association, New Orleans, LA.

APPENDIX
Sample Teacher Grow Reports®

The NYCDOE Class Report

USING ASSESSMENT TO HELP STUDENTS GROW

THE NEW YORK CITY DEPARTMENT OF EDUCATION

Dear Teacher,

Student assessment is most effective when the data is used to help inform instruction. The Department of Education is committed to providing resources to help you accomplish this goal.

This customized report provides insight into your current students' needs based on their performance on the city and state standardized exams taken in 2003–04.

Your own account on the web allows you to access teaching tools for each topic and individual student reports.

The Grow Network's materials have been developed to support *Children First* initiatives to help all children achieve in reading, writing, and mathematics.

We hope this report will help provide the data and tools you need to meet the needs of all your students.

Yours truly,

JOEL I. KLEIN

YOUR CURRENT STUDENTS' 2003–04 STANDARDIZED TEST RESULTS

For the
Math Teacher of:

Grade **9**
Class **901**
Subject **Math**
School **98X025**
Current School Year **2004–05**

INSIDE THIS REPORT

1 How did my students do?

2 What do they need to learn?

3 What tools are on the web?

Your personal **Login ID** and **Password** are inside.

www.grownetwork.com

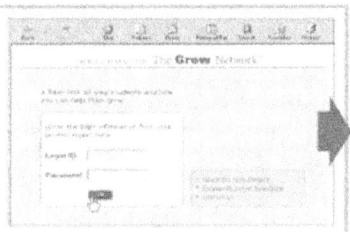

APPENDIX *(continued)*

How did my students do?

OVERALL SCORES FOR GRADE 8 STUDENTS [*]

Far Below Standards LEVEL 1: 517-680	Scale Score	Below Standards LEVEL 2: 681-715	Scale Score	Above Standards LEVEL 3: 716-759	Scale Score	Far Above Standards LEVEL 4: 760-862	Scale Score
Adams, Anita	677	Gazda, Janet	706	Allsopp, Victoria	752	Miller, James	775
Navarez, Esteben	674	Munoz, Maria	706	Cass, Mary	748	Davis, Latoyah	772
Rosado, Juan	670	Allen, John	705	Bochamps, Martin	744		
Tripp, Shannon	647	Roberts, Mike	696	Cavanaugh, Kate	744		
Ormond, Nancy	624	Cass, Aria	690	Chester, Jane	744		
		Crowe, Amir	687	Henderson, Paul	737		
		Nunez, Sunny	687	Jacobs, Danielle	722		
		Reese, Nelson	687				
		Gottlieb, Mati	683				
		Hernandez, Miguel	683				
		Smith, Tonya	681				

[*] *The results and recommendations shown on the right are based on the 16 Grade 9 students listed above who took the citywide Grade 8 test as Grade 8 students in the 2003–04 school year.*

LEARN MORE ABOUT EACH STUDENT:
Your web account contains Individual Student Reports with results and recommendations broken down by topic.

APPENDIX *(continued)*

What do they need to learn?

How my students did in each standard on the Grade 8 test

New York State Key Ideas	This Group	All NYC Students
Average % of Items Correct		
Mathematical Reasoning	37%	47%
Number and Numeration	55%	43%
Operations	44%	51%
Modeling/Multiple Representation	41%	43%
Measurement	33%	41%
Uncertainty	42%	53%
Patterns and Functions	40%	47%

These results are for students who were promoted last year. You can access results and recommendations for the students repeating this grade on your web account.

Recommendations for what they need to learn in Grade 9 based on last year's test

Help with Fundamentals [*]
- **Mathematical Reasoning**
  - Problem-Solving Strategies
- **Measurement**
  - Units of Time, Measure, Perimeter, Area, and Volume
  - Organizing and Interpreting Data
- **Uncertainty**
  - Estimation and Probability

Additional Instruction and Practice [**]
- **Operations**
  - Computations – Integers, Fractions, and Decimals
  - Basic Operations – Problem Solving
- **Modeling/Multiple Representation**
  - Properties of Geometric Shapes
  - Writing and Solving Equations
- **Patterns/Functions**
  - Patterns and Functions
  - Rate, Ratio, and Proportion

Advanced Work [***]
- **Number and Numeration**
  - Real Numbers and Arithmetic

[*] In the listed topics more of your students scored similarly to NYC students who scored at Level 1 on the test.
[**] In the listed topics most of your students scored similarly to NYC students who scored in Levels 2 and 3 on this test.
[***] In the listed topics more of your students scored similarly to NYC students who scored in Level 4 on this test.

A NOTE ON USING DATA THOUGHTFULLY
A single exam can provide only limited information. Review classroom assessments and student work to confirm these results and to observe your students' growth.

FIND YOUR CUSTOMIZED TOOLS AT www.grownetwork.com

- *Teaching Tools for Each Topic*
- *Individual Student Reports*
- *Flexible Groupings for Differentiated Instruction*
- *Class Roster Updated Throughout the Year*

Your Login ID and Password:

| Login ID | Sample |
| Password | Sample |

APPENDIX *(continued)*

What tools are on the web?

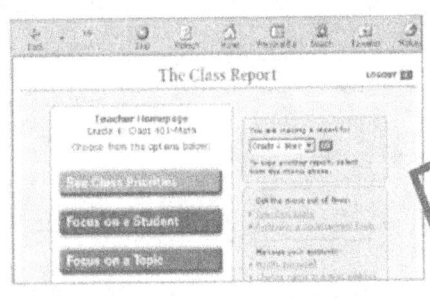

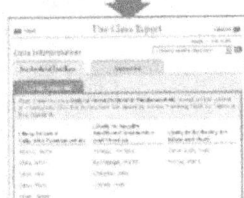
Flexible Groupings for your class

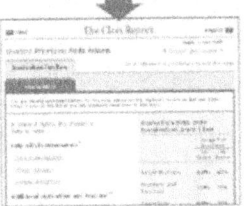
Individual Student Reports

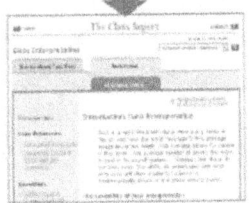
Teaching Tools for each topic

Children First: A New Agenda for Public Education in New York City is a multiyear program instituted by Mayor Bloomberg and Chancellor Klein. The goal of Children First is to create a system of outstanding schools in which effective teaching and learning is a reality for every teacher and child.

The new instructional approach of Children First has three major components:

- A comprehensive curriculum that provides a strong foundation for students' learning in reading, writing, and math.
- Additional books and materials in every school, including expanded classroom libraries for kindergarten through ninth grade.
- Enhanced professional development, including the assignment of trained literacy and math coaches, to support teachers in their classroom instruction.

Log on to your web account for ideas about using Grow resources to complement the Children First initiatives. Go to **www.nycenet.edu/childrenfirst** to learn more about Children First.

ABOUT THE GROW NETWORK *The Grow Network's goal is to transform assessment into opportunities for meaningful instruction. We provide teachers, school leaders, and parents with the data and tools they need to identify children's needs and help each child grow.*

Using Student-Assessment Results to Improve Instruction: Lessons From a Workshop

Richard J. Murnane, Nancy S. Sharkey,
and Kathryn P. Boudett
*Harvard Graduate School of Education
Harvard University*

The student-assessment results that schools must report to satisfy No Child Left Behind (NCLB) requirements could be useful in pinpointing strengths and weaknesses in instructional programs and students' skills. However, many school staffs lack the expertise to learn from assessment results. We describe lessons learned from a yearlong workshop aimed at helping 10 schools with this crucial work. Attended by school-based teams consisting of teachers, administrators, and graduate students in education, the workshop (a) explored different types of data and data analyses and (b) helped teams use data to analyze a school-specific problem and create an action plan. Lessons we learned include: schools need (a) a process for engaging in conversations around teaching and learning, (b) an opportunity for support of analyses of data from their school, and (c) leadership committed to the endeavor. Many participating school teams learned lessons from student-assessment results with important implications for instructional improvement.

Are particular middle school math teachers especially effective in teaching certain topics? As part of the yearlong workshop on learning from student-assessment results described in this article, a team from Boston's McCormack Middle School set out to answer this question. The team found that the school did have "in-house" topic experts whose students outperformed the state average on certain subsets of questions on the state eighth-grade math exam. The students of one teacher excelled on questions dealing with graphs; for another teacher, it was fractions; for a

---

Requests for reprints should be sent to Richard J. Murnane, Harvard Graduate School of Education, Gutman 469, Cambridge, MA 02138. E-mail: richard_murnane@harvard.edu

third, pre-algebra topics. Interviews with the teachers revealed that they were aware of their teaching strengths and could describe specific strategies they used to teach these topics. A consequence of the workshop team's findings was that the math teachers decided to focus professional development in the next year on teaching each other their best practices.

The McCormack School story illustrates that careful analysis of student-assessment results can help schools plan instructional improvements. This work is becoming increasingly important as schools work to satisfy the annual yearly progress (AYP) requirement of the No Child Left Behind (NCLB) legislation, yet learning from student-assessment results is an important activity in relatively few schools. Obstacles include lack of time, expertise, support, and understanding of the potential value of this activity (see Sharkey & Murnane, 2003).

During the 2002–2003 school year, we taught a workshop aimed at helping teams from 10 Boston public schools (BPS) to overcome some of these obstacles. The workshop, jointly sponsored by the Harvard Graduate School of Education (HGSE) and the BPS, was a new endeavor inspired by a desire to help schools make use of new software (MyBPS Assessments) that the BPS central office and its external partner, the Boston Plan for Excellence, had created. This user-friendly, Web-based software allows teachers and administrators to examine student-assessment results online, including item-level scores and test questions from the state's mandatory English/language arts (ELA) and mathematics exams.

We learned many lessons during the year about (a) how to structure a workshop that allows teachers and administrators to make constructive use of student assessment results, (b) what participating teachers and administrators find valuable in such a workshop, and (c) how a workshop might contribute to changes in school practices. Although we would not assert that our workshop is necessarily the best way to help school-based educators make constructive use of student-assessment results, we believe that the lessons we learned are relevant to other initiatives aimed at helping teachers and administrators do this potentially fruitful work. This article begins with a description of context, then provides a brief description of the workshop design, and finally discusses each of these types of lessons in turn.

DEFINITIONS AND CONTEXT

Educators use student-assessment results in at least three ways. They may adopt an *instrumental* approach, using the results to make decisions, for example, about which students will be required to attend summer school (Shadish, Cook, & Leviton, 1991; Thompson, 1994; Turnbull, 1998). Educators base these decisions directly on test-score data without considering why test scores are low. A second use of data is *symbolic*, either to justify a decision that has already been made or to support a predetermined stance (Feldman & March, 1981; Huberman, 1987; Patton, 1997). An example of this might be citing low test scores in a proposal for obtaining a grant for a particular project. A third use is *conceptual*, using results from summative and formative assessments to enrich dialog about what students know, what they are able to do, and how effective instruction has been (Weiss, 1977). In this approach, educators recognize that there may be many explanations for patterns in assessment results. Consequently, identifying patterns is only a first step, to be followed by systematic exploration of possible explanations. Often this requires collection and examination of other data, such as student writing samples and student attendance patterns. This conceptual approach to using student-assessment results follows closely the ideas of W. Edwards Deming, who developed strategies for improving quality control in businesses (Deming, 1982). Our workshop is based on the premise that the most valuable—and underutilized—use of student-assessment data is conceptual.

THE MASSACHUSETTS COMPREHENSIVE ASSESSMENT OF SKILLS (MCAS)

The BPS administer parts of the statewide Massachusetts Comprehensive Assessment of Skills (MCAS) in Grades 3 through 8 and Grade 10.[1] In addition, 10th-graders who do not pass the MCAS may retake the exam. The MCAS is an untimed test that includes multiple-choice, short-answer, and extended-response questions in mathematics, ELA, and science.

School staffs receive MCAS data by student (in an item-by-item analysis of multiple-choice questions, including all of the student's responses to all MCAS questions, whether the student's answer was correct, and the correct answer). This student-by-student analysis enables school faculties to compare their students' answers to the answers of students throughout the district and state. Schools also receive students' raw scores, scaled scores, and proficiency levels.

All MCAS questions are available on the Massachusetts' MCAS Web site soon after the test is administered. Students' written responses to the ELA open-ended questions also are available to school staffs (although these are provided electronically), with writing samples demonstrating the quality of writing represented by each possible score (1–4).

---

[1]Not all subjects are included at each grade level. English is assessed in Grades 3, 4, 7, and 10; math is assessed in Grades 4, 6, 8, and 10. Science and technology/engineering, as well as history and social science, are administered in Grades 5, 8, and 10.

BOSTON PUBLIC SCHOOLS (BPS)

Since Thomas Payzant became superintendent in 1995, the BPS have been engaged in a systemic reform effort aimed at improving the literacy and math skills of all students. One element of the reform effort is ongoing investment in professional development focused on improving literacy and math instruction. Another is providing schools with the tools to look regularly and systematically at student work.

One of the tools available to schools is MyBPS, the district's online data system. Through MyBPS, schools have access to basic student information (e.g., class schedule and whether the student is a second language learner). MyBPS also contains student MCAS results. MyBPS can be used to easily generate multiple analyses of item-level MCAS assessment data. Through graphical presentations of test results, linked to the actual test questions, teachers can readily see which questions students did well on and which questions posed greater difficulty for students. Notably, MyBPS also enables teachers to look at instructionally relevant groups of students. For example, if a school has a homework club that draws from students across classes, the school staff can easily select and examine the results of students in that club. Finally, test data are available to teachers and administrators.

Our workshop thus took place in a district that had both readily available student-assessment data and educators with a desire to use them.

THE WORKSHOP

Participants. After consultation with the course instructors, Superintendent Payzant invited the nine school principals who were part of his leadership group to send teams to the workshop. The logic was that these cluster leaders would be in a good position to share lessons from the workshop with the groups, or clusters, of schools under their leadership. Six cluster leaders chose to send teams. An additional four teams were recruited from schools that serve as internship sites for HGSE students. All of the BPS participants were volunteers; most were active in their school's Instructional Leadership Team (ILT). One incentive for BPS participants to commit to doing the work for the course was that they received HGSE course credit for completing the workshop. This credit counted toward fulfillment of state requirements for continuing professional development.

Team membership varied, but most teams consisted of an administrator (a principal or a director of instruction) and one to three teachers. In addition, 10 HGSE students, experienced teachers preparing to be school principals or teacher leaders, chose to enroll in the course. Each worked on one of the school-based teams, helping to answer the data-related question that the team posed for its school.

Participants varied markedly in their knowledge about analysis of student-assessment results. Many participants had never looked at the questions asked on the

MCAS. Others had read the exam questions but had not considered what might be learned from students' responses. Very few had looked for patterns in student-assessment results for several years. Additionally, schools varied in whether or not they had standing groups dedicated to managing and analyzing schoolwide assessment data the year before participating in the workshop. Although a few schools began the course already having highly functional data groups, most had either informal data groups or no groups at all.

The teaching team. Three instructors formed the instructional core of the teaching team. The team was led by an economics professor at the HGSE who had spent a year working in the BPS central office on issues of data use and school reform. He was assisted by two teaching fellows, both former public school teachers. One had studied how and why teachers in Boston used student-assessment data and had also assisted the staff of one Boston high school in its efforts to learn from assessment information. The other had experience as a professional developer for teachers. Both teaching fellows were advanced doctoral students in education at Harvard.

This team was aided and strengthened by a wider group of individuals who participated in the workshop and attended debriefing sessions after each workshop meeting. In these debriefing sessions, the team discussed issues of pedagogy and content and brainstormed ways to improve the course for each subsequent meeting. Participants in these debriefing meetings brought a broad variety of expertise and experiences to the teaching team, including technology expertise, school leadership experience, and experience as professional developers and researchers examining issues of school reform and data use in BPS.

Design. The workshop met for fourteen 2.5-hr sessions during the 2002–2003 school year, with all but two sessions held in a Boston high school. One goal was to familiarize participants with the steps involved in the conceptual use of data, including finding patterns and puzzles, identifying a central question, and designing and implementing a strategy to answer the question.[2] We recognized that some schools already possessed the capacity for data analysis. By including school-based teams in the class, however, we hoped to increase the building-level capacity for this type of work in all schools. We also hoped that by including elementary, middle, and high schools, teachers and administrators might be able to share lessons learned.

---

[2]When creating the syllabus, we drew on three sources. First, we drew on our own earlier research in Boston (Sharkey & Murnane, 2003). In this research, we asked teachers to describe how they used data, as well as what might help them use data better. Teachers identified professional development as a critical, yet missing, piece. Second, we attended meetings with BPS central office staff in which we learned what the district expected of schools with regard to data use and reporting. Third, we reviewed the literature on using data for school improvement. In this review, we included articles describing both practical and theoretical concerns. Copies of the complete syllabus are available from the authors on request.

The pedagogy for developing these data-related skills was to engage the group in the discussion of six cases, which had been created as practical exercises for school data teams to participate in during the course. Each case was written to focus on a particular aspect of the work. For example, the first case, "Harrison High School," described a school with a challenging student population and a reputation for poor performance. The challenge was to sift through student-assessment results to identify promising aspects of student performance, troubling aspects, and potential questions to explore. The cases were supplemented by readings that provided lessons about learning from student-assessment data. For example, one of the class favorites was *Inside the Black Box: Raising Standards Through Classroom Assessment* (Black & Wiliam, 1998). Prior to each session, participants wrote brief memos describing lessons learned from the readings and case studies dealing with challenges in learning from student-assessment results.

A second goal of the workshop was to help each school-based team to define and answer a question important to its school community. Each team wrote two reports. The first, submitted in November and revised in December, described the question the group asked and its strategy for answering it. The second, submitted in April and revised in May, described what the team learned in addressing its question and discussed how the results would be translated into instructional improvements. Each team gave a presentation of its findings to the workshop. Participants were then expected to incorporate feedback from the class into a revised presentation to give to their school leadership teams.

Data sources for this article. We used a variety of data sources in writing this report. These included the writings of workshop participants (individual weekly memos and the reports that school-based teams prepared) and notes from the debriefing sessions the teaching team held after each class to discuss what had worked well, what had not, and what the implications were for future sessions. We also asked participants to complete an online survey at the end of the year that asked for ratings of readings, cases, projects, and other aspects of the workshop. The survey contained both open- and close-ended questions. Of the 32 participants, 28 completed the survey. Finally, in our last workshop session, we asked participants to report on something that they had learned in the workshop. Analysis of the information from these varied sources revealed some striking patterns and helped us to identify key lessons learned by both the instructors and participants in the course.

LESSONS ABOUT HOW TO STRUCTURE THE WORKSHOP

Providing support for effective group work. Many of the groups that included administrators, teachers, and Harvard graduate students did not initially function well. We found that group members were often uncomfortable when discussing teacher and student work; members were also inexperienced in finding ways to include all group members in the inquiry process. A few individuals tended to dominate the conversations, leaving others to feel defensive or simply left out of the discussion. We found a solution to this problem in structured approaches to conversation. Participants found particularly valuable the question formulation technique developed by the Right Question Project[3] and a tuning protocol developed by the Coalition for Essential Schools.[4] Both of these tools provide structured ways to engage in conversations, ensuring that each participant has an equal voice in discussions and the decision-making process. For example, the question formulation technique stipulates that in brainstorming sessions, participants can only make suggestions (not evaluate them), and a scribe must write down each suggestion using the language in which it was made, not rephrasing it. This markedly reduces the likelihood that particular individuals will dominate the conversation. The tuning protocol, designed as a way to facilitate conversations about written work and projects, similarly tries to provide a forum for putting all ideas on the table before they are discussed, and keeps the conversation focused on the work being discussed, not on the presenter. As one student noted in reflecting upon the question formulation technique, "The method we used in class prevented the usual confrontations associated with different opinions."

Focusing on school-based data. Harvard graduate students found it stimulating to devote class time to discussing cases we had prepared to highlight particular challenges in learning from student-assessment results. However, most BPS teachers and administrators found this activity frustrating. In the words of one:

> I'm still struggling with how we might make the work even more authentic by using our actual schools. It seems like case study is an effective method for developing a common language and for simulating real life, but we also have many real life examples at our fingertips, and I wonder if we don't need a different process in a class that explicitly links theory and practice.

Devoting class time to working on school data projects. To encourage cross-fertilization of ideas, we initially separated members of school-based teams in forming groups for all workshop activities. Although participants reported that they did learn from participants from other schools, they explained that schedules and unexpected demands made it very difficult for them to find times to meet and

---

[3] For information on the Right Question Project and the structured approach to question formulation that it developed, see http://www.rightquestion.org.

[4] Information on the tuning protocol is available at http://www.nsrfharmony.org/protocol/doc/tuning.rtf and at http://www.essentialschools.org/cs/resources/view/ces_res/54.

discuss their joint work outside of class. As the year progressed, we found that the school teams particularly valued workshop time set aside for them to focus on their data projects.

Providing a forum for sharing ideas. As one participant noted in the year-end survey, "Sharing problems and insights with other schools gave us a broader insight." By pairing schools by grade level, school teams could receive feedback from peers who were facing the same issues. One participant commented, "Particularly helpful were presentations on learning results from middle school math for the middle school teams. Because we have a Grade 6 for the first time at our school, we knew early on what we needed to focus on."

LESSONS ABOUT WHAT PARTICIPANTS FIND VALUABLE IN A WORKSHOP

Understanding the potential of data to improve instruction. In one sense, learning from student-assessment results is nothing new to most educators. Good teachers have always assessed the skills of their students periodically and used the results to inform instruction. However, the idea that systematic analysis of results on externally imposed exams could provide information that is useful in planning instruction was new to most participants. Helping them to appreciate this was a contribution of the workshop that many participants emphasized. As one participant reported, "It has focused our attention on data and how it can be used to support instruction. It has helped us to know how to ask the right questions or at least ask questions concerning student progress based on data."

An administrator commented:

> I learned so many things: the real purpose of an ILT; beginning methods for taking apart MCAS data; how to state a problem, form a hypothesis, and discuss possible reasons for the problem; how different schools interact with the data; what my role as the instructional leader is; how powerful MCAS data is.

Exploring structured approaches to data-based problem solving. Participants valued opportunities to learn about how a number of different authors (e.g., Bernhardt, 2004; Love, 2002; North Central Regional Educational Laboratory, 2000[1]) described the steps of the problem-solving cycle and the key tools to use at each step (e.g., pattern analysis, disaggregation by student groups, flow charts, and root cause diagrams). Participants especially appreciated opportunities

---

[1] This document has been revised, and is now available as Learning Points Associates, 2004.

to apply these approaches to the data-related question their data team was addressing. One student summed it up: "I learned a variety of ways ... to generate questions by looking at data, and how best to come up with action steps and goals."

Looking beyond student test scores. Many participants reported that an early course assignment to take the complete MCAS under test conditions was particularly valuable. Here the "data" the students gathered were not test-score results but an understanding of the structure and content of the assessment itself. In the words of one participant:

> My greatest lesson learned through taking the test is that success on the MCAS is an all-school responsibility and this does not mean that students should drill math problems during physical education. What it means is that each discipline should identify skills and strategies that are important when taking any high-stakes test. These skills should be practiced in all disciplines. ... In science, [the focus] may be how number sense and operations are integral to physics; in foreign language, it is how active reading strategies are applicable to reading challenging texts in all languages. Teaching kids to use their minds well is an all-school effort and therefore the MCAS should be an all-school responsibility.

School teams identified many other sources of useful data. One team used surveys of parents to assess the value of a new format for parent-teacher conferences. Another catalogued the types and frequency of writing assignments the teachers in their school gave. A third compiled a list of failing students and interviewed teachers about these students: "not just the math teacher, but all the teachers." A fourth analyzed curriculum materials to explore why students were performing poorly on very specific types of questions on the MCAS.

Allowing questions to evolve. The questions teams pursued were as varied as the data sources they investigated. Regular exposure to different schools' approaches helped broaden participants' sense of possibilities. Two middle school teams examined why their schools' students performed less well on the MCAS math exam than on the MCAS ELA exam. One high school team explored whether a student's grade point average (GPA) was a strong predictor of performance on the MCAS. Another asked whether students' performances on MCAS questions dealing with some math topics were improving from year to year while scores on questions dealing with other math topics were not. One team set out to understand why Asian American students in their high school did not score well on the MCAS exam. The team learned that these students' GPAs did not predict their MCAS scores. This led them to explore whether the GPAs of other students predicted MCAS scores well.

Learning that this was not the case, the team refocused its attention on grading practices in the school.

LESSONS ABOUT HOW A WORKSHOP MIGHT CONTRIBUTE TO CHANGES IN SCHOOL PRACTICES

The key research question when evaluating a workshop such as this one is whether participation led to the planning of instructional improvements that were then implemented. At this point, we have data only on the first step in this process: the extent to which school teams used data to plan instructional change. Our data reveal that the course may have contributed to changing school practice in several ways.

Offering a structure for achieving school goals. Participants at three schools reported that their data teams were more functional at the end of the course than the teams had been in the year before participating. For these schools, participation in the course may have helped institutionalize data work. Participants reported that deadlines for first drafts and for revised drafts pushed data teams to meet, make decisions, develop analysis plans, and describe what they found. The requirement to read and write about the reports prepared by other schools provided insights that many school teams valued.

Participants reported sharing with their school colleagues many activities and tools that they learned about in the workshop. For example, several schools allocated professional development time to discussing the questions on the MCAS. Participants also reported taking back to their schools the group facilitation techniques used in the workshop, which they then used with their colleagues. In the words of one participant: "The process of having the discussion is just as important as the substance ... especially when the stakes are so high."

One participant commented that the data his team generated were useful in documenting a problem teachers had already identified, namely, that the math curriculum was not well aligned with the MCAS. By showing that one third of the MCAS sixth-grade math exam made use of algebra and that the middle school math curriculum did not teach the relevant tools until the seventh grade, the data team was able to garner support for teaching certain algebra skills during the sixth grade. He wrote of the teachers' renewed optimism: "They had pretty much given up on the idea of it [the disconnect between the test and the curriculum] being fixed. Now that there were concrete data to support these claims, they are optimistic that the appropriate changes will be made." Thus, exploring data may lead to a validation of teachers' perceptions and create impetus for change.

Encouraging linking data analysis to instructional improvements. In planning the workshop, we expected that the most difficult challenge for school teams would be making the link to improving instruction. To our surprise, this turned out not to be the case for some schools. As illustrated by McCormack's plans for professional development, school-based teams had a variety of creative ideas for making constructive use of new knowledge about what students in their schools were learning and not learning.

For other school teams, the link to instruction was more elusive, and the intention to "game the system" seemed to take precedence over making constructive changes in how students were taught. We observed this in teams working in high schools where the MCAS scores of almost half of the 10th-graders were below the minimum scores required for high school graduation. Understandably, these educators felt enormous pressure to increase the number of students who passed the exams. This led them to focus their attention on students whose scores fell just below the minimum passing score and to analyze what types of questions these students answered incorrectly. We were uncomfortable with this focus because it appeared to be aimed primarily at improving test-taking skills rather than improving students' writing, reading comprehension, and understanding of key math concepts.

Building appreciation of the critical role of leadership. As one participant noted, "I have learned the importance of [having] the leadership of a building step up and model the importance of looking at the data." The school principal at the McCormack School, a strong advocate of data analysis, embraced the findings of the data team's project and worked with the school's math teachers to plan how to make use of their findings. Strong leadership support was also present at other schools that were able to make an explicit link between data analysis and instruction.

In contrast, at another school, evidence that students' GPAs were not good predictors of MCAS scores—a finding that might have been a catalyst for an important faculty discussion about grading practices—fell on barren ground because the school principal did not see data analysis as important. Lack of support from school leadership meant that the team's work was not likely to make a difference in school practices.

Participants also noted a new appreciation for the role the principal plays in setting a tone for the school. One participant, an HGSE student, said, "It gave me a peek at how incredibly challenging a role of a principal is in getting staff to see this as important, especially [teachers of] those grades that don't take the test."

CONCLUSION

A result of NCLB is that virtually every child in the nation's public schools will take standardized reading and math tests every year. If the tests are well designed and aligned with states' learning standards, a great deal can be learned from the assessment results that can guide instructional improvements. This is especially the case when these data are used in conjunction with formative test results, as well as with the wide range of other information about students that is available to most schools. However, the requisite work is new for most of the nation's educators. Relatively few have experience in examining student-assessment results systematically, the time to do it, and access to user-friendly software to do the work efficiently. Our yearlong workshop convinced us that school-based educators need a variety of supports to make constructive use of student-assessment results.

New versions of the workshop incorporating many of the changes suggested by participants were offered in the 2003–2004 and 2004–2005 academic years, in the hope of providing even more useful supports to school-based educators.

REFERENCES

Bernhardt, V. L. (2004). *Data analysis for comprehensive school improvement* (2nd ed.). Larchmont, NY: Eye on Education.

Black, P., & Wiliam, D. (1998). Inside the black box: Raising standards through classroom assessment." *Phi Delta Kappan, 80,* 139–144, 146–148. Retrieved November 30, 2004, from http://www.pdkintl.org/kappan/kbla9810.htm

Deming, W. E. (1982). *Out of the crisis.* Cambridge, MA: MIT Press.

Feldman, M., & March, J. (1981). Information in organizations as signal and symbol. *Administrative Science Quarterly, 26,* 171–186.

Huberman, M. (1987). Steps toward an integrated model of research utilization. *Knowledge, 8,* 586–611.

Learning Points Associates (2004). *Guide to using data in school improvement efforts: A compilation of knowledge from data retreats and data use at Learning Points Associates.* Naperville, IL: Author. Retreived April 8, 2005, from http://www.ncrel.org/datause/howto/guidebook.pdf

Love, N. (2002). *Using data/getting results: A practical guide for school improvement in mathematics and science.* Norwood, MA: Christopher-Gordon.

Patton, M. (1997). *Utilization-focused evaluation* (3rd ed.). Thousand Oaks, CA: Sage.

Shadish, W., Cook, T., & Leviton, L. (1991). *Foundations of program evaluation: Theories of practice.* Newbury Park, CA: Sage.

Sharkey, N. S., & Murnane, R. J. (2003). Learning from student assessment results: A necessary, if difficult, response to NCLB. *Educational Leadership, 61*(3), 77–82.

Thompson, B. (1994, April). *The revised program evaluation standards and their correlation with the evaluation use literature.* Paper presented at the annual meeting of the American Educational Research Association, New Orleans, LA.

Turnbull, B. (1998). A confirmatory factor analytic model of evaluation use. *The Canadian Journal of Program Evaluation, 13*(2), 75–87.

Weiss, C. (1977). Research for policy's sake: The enlightenment function of social research. *Policy Analysis, 3,* 531–545.

Using Data Mining to Identify Actionable Information: Breaking New Ground in Data-Driven Decision Making

Philip A. Streifer
Department of Educational Leadership
Neag School of Education, University of Connecticut

Jeffrey A. Schumann
Principal, Martin Kellogg Middle School
Newington, Connecticut

The implementation of No Child Left Behind (NCLB) presents important challenges for schools across the nation to identify problems that lead to poor performance. Yet schools must intervene with instructional programs that can make a difference and evaluate the effectiveness of such programs. New advances in artificial intelligence (AI) data-mining software can aid in identifying important indexes of achievement to help teachers and administrators improve these instructional and programmatic interventions. The problem addressed in this study is the difficulty that school leaders face in using the stores of data they have already collected to analyze the effectiveness of interventions focused on improving achievement. The essential question is whether educators can predict student achievement from all of the disparate variables already stored in typical data warehouses. Support for this study was provided by SPSS, Inc., a partner in the research, who provided the University of Connecticut with several licenses for its premier data-mining application—Clementine 8.5.

Traditional analytics can neither easily nor systematically handle the complexities of school data to address the queries school leaders have about achievement, an-

---

Requests for reprints should be sent to Philip A. Streifer, Department of Educational Leadership, Neag School of Education, University of Connecticut, 249 Glenbrook Road Unit 2093, Storrs, CT 06269–2093. E-mail: streifer@edsmartinc.com

nual yearly progress (AYP), and interventions that work. To answer such questions, we need to utilize school input, process (instructional and programmatic), and output variables in one analysis. Data stored in data warehouses (databases designed to store huge amounts of historical data employing special design structures that require additional tools to access) take the form of three typologies: (a) student input variables such as gender, race, and socioeconomic status; (b) variables that describe the process of schooling, such as courses taken, the teachers of those courses, and special programs in which students have participated; and (c) output measures of the educational process, such as test scores and class grades. These non-normative variables are of multiple types: range, ordinal, discrete, and text. The goal of data mining is to use all of these measures in one analysis to develop a comprehensive and accurate model to predict student achievement by identifying the contributors to that achievement from among myriad historical variables already collected that represent the stored totality of a student's school experience. Data-mining applications have yet to be applied to the problems of school leadership and decision making, although they are widely and successfully used in the private sector.

The existence of an achievement gap in this country is well known. No Child Left Behind (NCLB) was enacted to shed light on those student groups whose performance on measures of academic achievement is lagging. But typical NCLB analyses conducted by school districts (Streifer, 2002, 2004b) do not help school leaders determine which interventions, from among the entirety of school experiences, most contribute to school success. Predictive analytics are needed for such analyses, but historical school data are disparate; that is, they take the form of non-normative variables that are reported along a wide range of score types, as previously mentioned. It is impractical to transform all of these data elements prior to running traditional prediction analytics. For example, in a study to predict future reading difficulties in kindergartners, Catts, Fey, Zhang, and Tomblin (2001) ran into this very problem. They noted that, to use their predictive model, other researchers would have to transform new data into z scores to conform to their original normative data. This is impractical for everyday use by busy school leaders, even those with capable research departments. The purpose of our research was to (a) develop a process that can predict student achievement from among the disparate variables already stored in typical data warehouses, and (b) develop a replicable process to help school leaders design (or co-construct) better instructional and programmatic interventions.

BACKGROUND AND RATIONALE

It is important that we consider school leaders' most important questions about how to improve student achievement: They want to know if instructional programs are working, whether recent interventions are having any impact, and if student mobility is a significant factor in achievement, among other questions. Cost-benefit questions, such as whether early childhood or Reading Recovery programs work, are becoming more important. Accountability forces the consideration of questions like *What is the best predictor of our school's adequate yearly progress? Can the district intervene in time to have an impact?* and *Does the sequence of course experiences and teachers make a difference in achieving high standards on mastery tests?*

New artificial intelligence (AI) data-mining tools have capabilities that are more flexible than traditional statistical tools for dealing with complex questions and data sets. For example, consider the problem of predicting 10th-grade mastery test scores (for those 10th graders in 2004) from a host of data elements on these children going back to the 4th grade. These data elements represent multiple data types: discrete, ordinal, scale, and text. Traditional techniques, such as logistic or linear regression or discriminant function analysis, cannot handle this kind of complexity of data types in one single analysis, if at all, without significant modification or manipulation.

Taking the idea a step further, once the prediction model is run on this problem—even if this were possible with traditional statistical methods—it would not be possible to apply systematically the data-mining model created on the data from 10th graders in 2004 to subsequent cohorts of students who will be 10th graders in 2005, 2006, 2007, and so on, without significant transformations of the data. This is assuming that the data were normative to begin with, as demonstrated by Catts et al. (2001). This example clearly demonstrates that the benefits of data mining are the ability to (a) handle very complex data environments in one analysis and (b) systematically apply the results obtained from one cohort to predict the outcome from totally different cohorts with minimal or no data manipulation.

The educational value of the results allows one to say that, absent some additional intervention, students who will be X graders in Y years will perform at Z level. Moreover, if educators can identify the interventions or process variables that are strong predictors of success, the likelihood of positively impacting future achievement will be improved.

Data mining defined. Data mining is more than statistics: It is a process of problem identification, data gathering and manipulation, statistical/prediction modeling, and output display leading to deployment or decision making. Fundamental to this process is the ability to sort through and utilize the vast amounts of data already collected on students by districts and stored in data warehouses. A typical data warehouse, which contains all the data needed to run these analyses, would house several hundred data variables on each student for each year of schooling. Some data warehouses contain historical data going back 10 or even 20 years. Mining these data warehouses is an almost impossible task without the proper technologies. Because there is so much data collected, it is virtually impossible to know a priori what all of the interactions are or might be between and among these variables. The situation for the private sector is no different, as many organizations with data warehouses remain data rich and knowledge poor.

According to Han and Kamber (2001), the term *data mining* is misleading. The phrase *gold mining* refers to the search for gold in rocks or sand; data mining, however, is not a search for data. In fact, data mining has come into existence because of a surplus of data: Data mining is a search for information and knowledge. Data mining was described by Fuller (2002) as the application of rigorous statistical analysis to large masses of data in an effort to extract meaningful trends and patterns often hidden by the sheer volume and arrangement of the data. Other similar definitions were given by Hand, Mannila, and Smyth (2001), Ramachadran (2001), and Two Crows Corporation (1999).

To explore these vast stores of data, new techniques have been invented that permit the nature of the study to change. Instead of exploring a predetermined hypothesis, data mining is predominantly exploratory data analysis (EDA), in which there are no preset hypotheses. Data mining is the search for hidden relationships and patterns in the data that can add to one's understanding of organizational effectiveness. Thus, "data mining is the non-trivial extraction of implicit, previously unknown, interesting, and potentially useful information, usually in the form of knowledge patterns or models" (Chen, 2001, p. 12).

There are several approaches to the data-mining process, all basically similar in nature (Cegal, Roddick, & Calder, 2003; Han & Kamber, 2001; Two Crows, 1999). These models have evolved to the current data-mining process called the Cross-Industry Standard Process for Data Mining (CRISP-DM), which is deployed by SPSS in its Clementine software. The CRISP-DM process was used in this study, employing classification and regression tree (CART) methodology for predictive modeling. Details on the workings of CART methods and the CRISP-DM framework can be found in Breiman, Freidman, Olshen, and Stone (1984), Chapman et al. (1999), Feelders, Daniels, and Holsheimer (2000), Han and Kamber (2001), Parr Rud (2001), Thearling (1997), and Two Crows (1999).

The actual work of data mining is not all that different from traditional research approaches, as it requires the collection of and access to appropriate data, data clean-up and preparation, and proper analysis and interpretation. During the final phases of analysis and interpretation, there are more dramatic differences compared to traditional research methods because the primary interests in data mining are searching for hidden relationships and patterns and modeling.

The importance of domain knowledge. Data mining requires that its practitioners have enough domain knowledge to know whether revealed relationships are meaningful. Those who promote the use of these applications point out that it must be guided by individuals who know the business environment, have a thorough understanding of how the data are collected and stored, and possess at least a general knowledge of the analytical methodologies being used to produce the information (Dhar & Stein, 1997; McClean, Scotney, & Shapcott, 2000; Parr Rud, 2001; Ramachadran, 2001; Two Crows, 1999). Luan (2002) referred to this as *domain knowledge*, noting that it is a critical component of the data-mining process. "Unless the output of the data-mining system can be understood qualitatively, it won't be of any use" (Thearling, 1997, p. 2). In other words, for data mining to be useful, someone in the organization who possesses an understanding (domain knowledge) of both the organization and the process of data mining is needed to facilitate the interpretation of the data-mining results into language understandable and usable by others in decision-making positions. Domain knowledge may also reduce the chance of accepting skewed results derived from "missing or outlying data" (McClean et al., p. 545).

The essential difference between data mining and traditional statistical approaches becomes apparent when we consider this sample research question: Of all the variables collected in a data warehouse on children between kindergarten and seventh grade, what are the best predictors of seventh-grade reading on the Gates-MacGinitie Reading Test?

This question seeks to explore the relationships between and among all of the variables loaded into the data warehouse between kindergarten and seventh grade. This would include a wide variety of score types, from discrete and ordinal (such as gender and race) to various range test data reported on many different scales. We could even include teachers and the sequence of teachers that students had during these years. Districts often code program participation either as discrete variables (yes/no) or time variables that denote the degree of participation. All of this complexity makes for a challenging analysis. Although it might be possible to run separate traditional analyses to handle all of the data complexity, doing so would negate the primary purpose of the study: exploratory data analysis, in which there is no a priori set of hypotheses about how the data variables are related. Therefore, this question requires the application of data-mining techniques, employing one or more of the newly designed statistical algorithms. We used SPSS's Clementine and its CART algorithm for the analysis and interpretation of this question.

PREDICTING READING ACHIEVEMENT USING CRISP-DM

The study reported on here addressed a question that a New England suburban school superintendent had about achievement in her district. The specific question posed by this superintendent was: "What indicators in our data warehouse are the best predictors of success in reading comprehension as reported by the comprehension subtest [normal curve equivalent] NCE score on the seventh-grade Gates-MacGinitie Reading Test for the cohorts of students during 1998–2003?"[1]

There were hundreds of data elements available for analysis, so data extraction, manipulation, and analysis were a challenge. SPSS Clementine provides a utility for easing this process, described graphically as a *stream* (see Figure 1). A stream is a series of *nodes*, each of which performs a certain function from data gathering, to manipulation, to analysis, to presentation of the results. In Clementine, nodes are functions that the user wishes to perform, such as extracting data from the data warehouse or transforming the data into a flat file, and so on. The entire data manipulation process, along with the actual analysis, is performed on one screen in Clementine.

Developing a Clementine stream. Figure 1 shows a complete analysis stream for one cohort of this reading study, from extraction of the data from the data warehouse to the comparison of the actual and predicted dependant variable using correlation. All of the nodes in the stream feed information to the next node in the direction of the arrow connecting them.

At the far left of Figure 1 are 14 data tables extracted from the district's data warehouse, each containing many fields and hundreds of student records. They all feed their information to the Merge node, which looks for a common field on which the data from the 14 tables can be merged. In this case, Student ID is being used as the common field for merging the data. The next nodes in the stream are Type nodes: They are labeled *All Data* and *Academic Data*. Here the data manipulation functions are performed. Fields are selected as dependent and independent variables and prepared to be passed on to the analysis node. The data can be cleaned in this node as well. Issues of missing data and "dirty" data can be rectified in this node so that only clean data will be used in the analysis or mining model.

In this stream, we wanted to create two sets of independent variables, All Data and Academic Data, so we placed two type nodes in the stream. This versatility allows the user to explore a variety of data sets in the quest to produce the optimum model for the project at hand. A discussion of All Data versus Academic Data follows in a later section of this article.

Data fields used in the analysis. Of the original variables in all of the data tables shown in Figure 1, we selected the 24 most appropriate independent variables common across all three cohorts (2001, 2002, and 2003).

There are also several variables that the researchers decided not to use here that are nontest items: student gender, parent/guardian relationship, kindergarten expe-

---

[1]The data warehouse did not have all the data tables necessary to process all six years; the earliest three years were missing entire data sets needed for the analysis. Thus, the study was limited to the cohorts from 2001, 2002, and 2003.

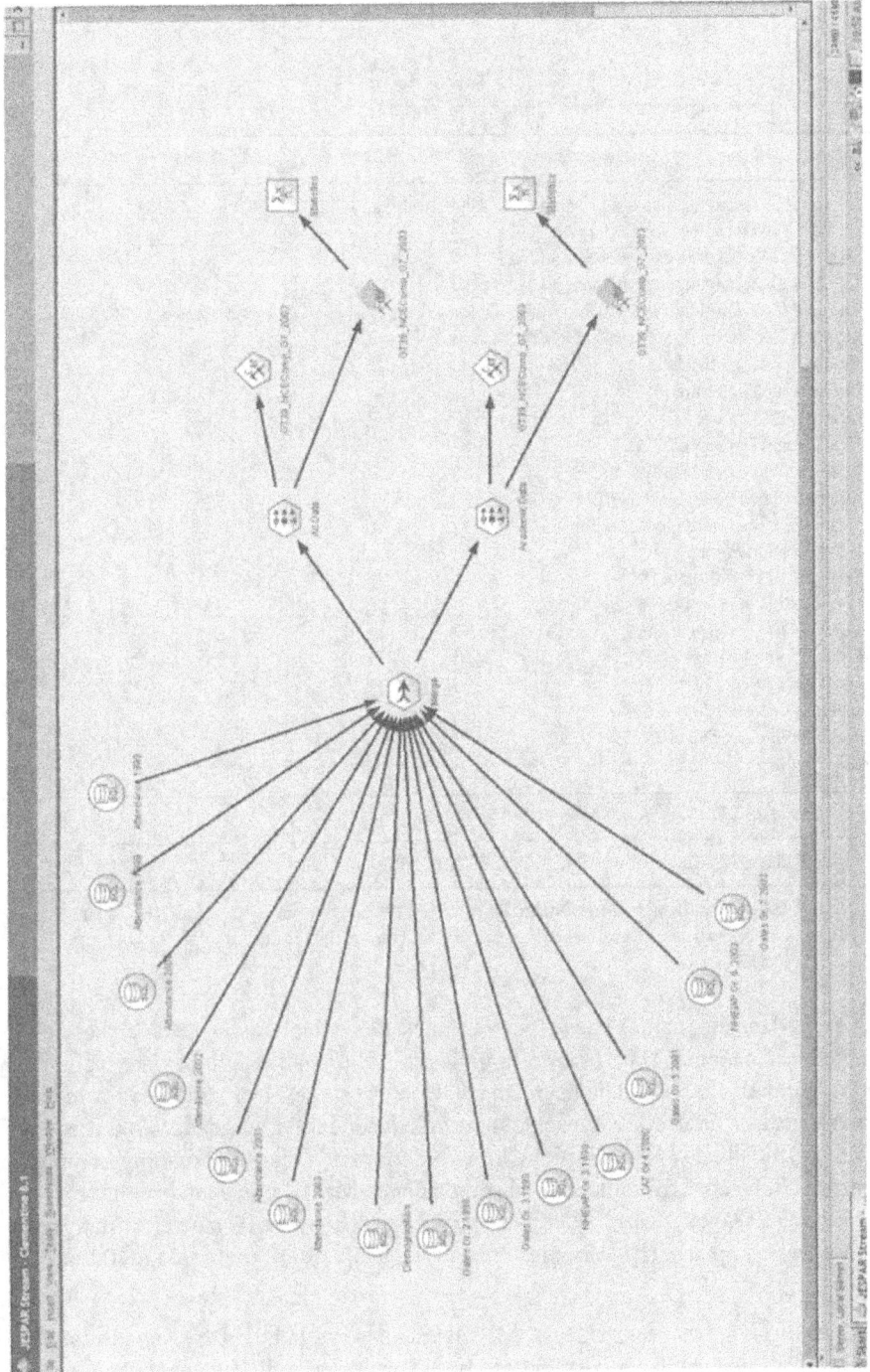

FIGURE 1 Clementine stream for data extraction, transofrmation, and analysis.

TABLE 1
Independent and Dependent Variables for Reading Study

Independent or Predictor Variables

    Attendance (expressed as a percentage) for 1998, 1999, and 2000
    Grade 4 CAT reading vocabulary NCE
    Grade 4 CAT reading comprehension NCE
    Grade 4 CAT language mechanics NCE
    Grade 4 CAT language expression NCE
    Grade 4 CAT math computation NCE
    Grade 4 CAT math concepts application NCE
    Grade 4 CAT spelling NCE
    Grade 4 CAT study skills NCE
    Grade 4 CAT science NCE
    Grade 4 CAT social studies NCE
    Grade 5 Gates vocabulary NCE
    Grade 5 Gates reading comprehension NCE
    Grade 6 NH language arts scale
    Grade 6 NH math scale
    Grade 6 NH social studies scale
    Grade 6 NH science scale
    Grade 6 NH writing raw
Student gender
Student parent/guardian relationship
Kindergarten experience
Teacher name

Dependent of Target Variable

    Grade 7 Gates Reading Comprehension NCE score

Note. CAT = California Achievement Test; NCE = Normal Curve Equivalent; NH = State Mastery Test. Items in italics are variables added for the All Data variable set.

rience, and teacher name. These four variables are not included in the analyses designated as Academic Data (shown in italics in Table 1) although they are included in the All data analysis. The user can easily select or deselect variables for inclusion in any one analysis. For each cohort, the dependent or target variable was the seventh-grade Gates-MacGinitie reading NCE score. This is the reading comprehension NCE score from the seventh-grade Gates-MacGinitie Test—with the designation GT39—as it was loaded into the data warehouse in its native format from the testing company. The variables used in the analysis are presented in Table 1.

Dealing with missing data. Missing data were handled by substituting a predicted value for missing data points, based on nonmissing data using the Neural Net predictive modeling technique.

Standard tree output of CART. When Clementine runs CART, it produces a tree that shows the sequence of clustering variables. When reviewed carefully, this tree holds in each segment of itself the variable name, the number of records that variable is based on, and other useful information. The tree is also a representation of the predictive model, the idea being that careful study of the output will reveal the relative strength of the variables.

Summarizing results for easier interpretation. Table 2 shows the results of the CART output tree summarized across the three cohorts analyzed. Each variable is listed and the cells represent the number of times that variable appeared on the tree for each cohort. From this, we can intuit how important each variable is in answering the superintendent's question.

Of the independent variables in the analysis, we can see in Table 2 just those that appear to be the most important across cohorts. Grade 4 is an important threshold year, as evidenced by the fact that reading vocabulary, reading comprehension, language mechanics, math concepts application, math computation, and study skills emerged as important predictor variables. Science in Grade 3 was particularly important for Cohort 2.

The administrative team reacted to this information in a very practical nature. Each began to articulate with more specificity areas of the curriculum that might be impacting these variables. An interesting, though not totally unexpected, finding was that the superintendent presented a longer range plan of interventions than did the assistant superintendent, who suggested additional resources be used to strengthen the curriculum delivered closer to the dependent variable.

TABLE 2
Summary of CART Output by Cohort

Data Fields	Cohort 1	Cohort 2	Cohort 3
CT 18 Reading vocabulary Grade 4	2	1	5
CT 22 Language expression Grade 4	2	3	2
GT 24 Science Grade 5	2	2	3
CT 19 Reading comprehension Grade 4	3	3	
CT 21 Language mechanics Grade 4	3	2	1
GT 24 Science Grade 3	1	4	
CT 25 Math concepts application Grade 4	1	3	
CT 30 Study skills Grade 4	2	1	1
GT 24 Science Grade 2	4		
CT 24 Math computation Grade 4	1	1	1
GT 23 Vocabulary Grade 5		2	1

Note. CT = California Achievement Test variable; GT = Gates-MacGinitie Test variable; CART = classification and regression tree algorithm.

TABLE 3
Correlation Between Predicted and Actual Dependent Variable

	All Data		Academic Data	
Cohort	Pearson r	R^2	Pearson r	R^2
Cohort 1: Grade 7 (2003)	0.883	0.779	0.855	0.731
Cohort 2: Grade 7 (2002)	0.824	0.678	0.806	0.649
Cohort 3: Grade 7 (2001)	0.871	0.758	0.876	0.76

TABLE 4
Correlation Between Predicted and Actual Reading
Comprehension Scores

	Pearson r	r^2
2001 Model predicting 2002	0.564	0.318
2001 Model predicting 2003	0.709	0.502

All Data versus Academic Data (using only test scores). As the study progressed, we became interested in knowing what would result if we separated out all of the demographic and teacher variables from just the test scores, hypothesizing that these variables were weaker and would result in fewer significant correlations between the actual and predicted scores. Even though the correlations for All Data were high to begin with, it was logical to assume that using better aligned independent variables would yield an even stronger model. However, that was not the case. In fact, using All Data did not appreciably weaken the model. The variables, such as student demographics and teacher sequence, lead to rich discussions and in some ways began to shed light on programmatic issues. We were pleased that Clementine's CART algorithm was robust enough to handle these variables.

Table 3 presents the correlational values for each cohort and shows the correlation between the predicted dependent variable with the actual dependent variable. The strong Pearson r values indicate that the CART algorithm created a closely aligned predicted value for each student when compared to the actual score.

Extending the study beyond the superintendent's question. The superintendent wanted to know which variables were the most important predictors of seventh-grade reading comprehension as expressed by the seventh-grade comprehension score on the Gates-MacGinitie Test. The previous analysis answered that question. Given that we had full data sets for each of the three cohorts, and given that data-mining applications can predict new cohort performance from a previous group, it was logical to test this out on the data sets. We applied the prediction model created by CART on the 2001 cohort to the other two cohorts. Table 4 shows the result of this analysis using All Data. The Pearson *r* represents the correlation between the actual score and the predicted score, which was created by applying the data-mining model created on the 2001 cohort to generate the predicted reading scores for the two new cohorts, 2002 and 2003.

We can see that in applying the 2001 prediction model to the two subsequent cohorts, the correlations are moderate. In a study predicting reading achievement in Grade 5 from kindergarten phonological awareness (PA) and naming speed (NS), Kirby, Parrila, and Pfeiffer (2003) used principal-axis factor analysis to identify the factors PA and NS, then hierarchical regression to predict the dependent variable. In the regression results, r^2 values were generally the same or lower. This is a preliminary indication that the results from data-mining applications are similar to, if not somewhat stronger than, traditional methods. It must be acknowledged that the purpose of Kirby et al.'s study was different: They were testing a specific hypothesis, whereas data mining is more appropriate for exploratory data analysis.

SIGNIFICANCE OF THE FINDINGS

There are three significant findings from this study. First, the complicated and often messy issue of data preparation (data extraction and manipulation) is often resolvable in Clementine.

Second, we can build data-mining models that produce a predicted target variable that is highly correlated to the actual target variable. Using these models in this particular study, we were able to identify the independent variables that appeared to be most important across all three cohorts. We also show that a predictive model built on one cohort can be applied to predict other cohorts with moderate correlational values. This study builds on previous work in which we demonstrated an ability to create a prediction model, although on a more limited data set (Streifer, 2004a).

Third, when presented with a revised summary of the CART output (not raw output), school administrators found this summary useful: The results confirmed their intuitive beliefs. Developing new and more easily understandable methods of presenting these results to school administrators will enhance their ability to make curriculum decisions that are strategically connected to future student achievement.

IMPLICATIONS AND FURTHER RESEARCH

The essential question at this juncture is: How excited should we be over these results? This is a question that we are frequently asked. In other words, how significant are these findings, and how useful will these techniques be for improving data-based decision making? At one level, we are hopeful that these applications and techniques will prove very useful. For example, the reading study presented here was not possible a year ago without incurring major costs for ongoing data manipulation, even with another fairly expensive data-mining application. SPSS's Clementine has proven itself extremely capable in this regard, but it, too, is a costly application with a serious learning curve required to obtain the results we have presented in this article. Regardless, we are heartened that the analysis can now be done in hours, not months.

As to the statistical power and significance of the findings, we are still cautious. More studies are needed to determine if these are spurious results—a result of very tightly aligned data elements in a suburban school district—or whether the techniques apply more universally. Subsequent studies now ongoing appear to indicate the latter; however, time will tell.

For now, we are moving forward with two major lines of research. One has to do with the use of text variables that are proxies or indicators for the quality of the schooling experience, such as course names and teacher names. We expect to report soon on a study in which we appear to be able to predict students' 11th-grade Scholastic Aptitude Test (SAT) scores solely from the courses (as denoted by course names) and sequence of courses they have taken through middle and high school. An extension of this work will be to build more robust value-added models that include a wider range of variables beyond just test scores. Our interest here surrounds the fact that we intuitively know that student achievement is the product of a sequence of experiences, not just the result of experiences with a single teacher or class. Thus, we are working on building prediction models that can accurately determine the impact that the sequences of student experiences have on achievement. A second line of work focuses on broadening the reading study reported on here to schools and school districts with a more diverse student body. Again, our preliminary work is promising. As part of this study, we are also working on developing clearer representations of the predictive models to aid in interpretation and decision making. In the final analysis, we are encouraged by these results and hopeful that these tools and techniques can be applied more universally once the costs of purchasing, implementing, and learning these new software packages are brought down and their methods of statistical analysis made more universally accessible to the end user or decision maker.

In summary, we are working to prove that the results found in the reading study reported on here can be more universally applied to a wide range of schools and school districts. We also seek to make the tools and output of such programs easier to use and more cost affordable. Accomplishing these goals will significantly contribute to the field of data-driven decision making, bringing to that field the power of predictive analytics.

REFERENCES

Breiman, L., Friedman, J. H., Olshen, R. A., & Stone, C. J. (1984). *Classification and regression trees.* Pacific Grove, CA: Wadsworth.
Catts, H., Fey, M., Zhang, X., & Tomblin, B. (2001). Estimating the risk of future reading difficulties in kindergarten children: A research-based model and its clinical implementation. *Language, Speech, and Hearing Services in Schools, 32,* 38–50.
Cegal, A., Roddick, J., & Calder, P. (2003). Guiding knowledge discovery through interactive data mining. In P. Pendharkar (Ed.), *Managing data mining technologies in organizations: Techniques and applications* (pp. 45–87). Hershey, PA: Idea Group Publishing.
Chen, Z. (2001). *Data mining and uncertain reasoning: An integrated approach.* New York: Wiley.
Chapman, P., Clinton, J., Kerber, R., Khabaza, T., Reinartz, T., Shearer, C., et al. (1999). *CRISP-DM: Step-by-step data mining guide.* Retrieved December 15, 2004, from http://www.crisp-dm.org/CRISPWP-0800.pdf
Dhar, V., & Stein, R. (1997). *Seven methods for transforming corporate data into business intelligence.* Upper Saddle River, NJ: Prentice Hall.
Feelders, A., Daniels, H., & Holsheimer, M. (2000). Methodological and practical aspects of data mining. *Information & Management, 37,* 271–281.
Fuller, D. (2002, October 11). *Data mining overview.* Retrieved December 15, 2004, from the DM Review Web site: http://www.datawarehouse.com/article/?articleId=3080&searchTerm=Data%20mining%20overview
Han, J., & Kamber, M. (2001). *Data mining: Concepts and techniques.* San Diego, CA: Morgan Kaufman.
Hand, D., Mannila, H., & Smyth, P. (2001). *Principles of data mining.* Cambridge, MA: MIT Press.
Kirby, J., Parrila, R., & Pfeiffer, S. (2003). Naming speed and phonological awareness as predictors of reading development. *Journal of Educational Psychology, 95,* 455–464.
Luan, J. (2002). *Data mining applications in higher education.* Retrieved January 7, 2003, from the Business Software Reviews Web site: http://www.spssbi.com
McClean, S., Scotney, B., & Shapcott, M. (2000). Incorporating domain knowledge into attribute-orientated data mining. *International Journal of Intelligent Systems, 15,* 535–547.
Parr Rud, O. (2001). *Data mining cookbook: Modeling data for marketing, risk, and customer relationship management.* New York: Wiley.
Ramachadran, P. (2001). *Mining for gold* (White Paper). Retrieved December 6, 2002, from the Wipro Technologies Web site: http://www.wipro.com/dwlphp/savetragetas.php3?pdf=wipro_mining_for_gold.pdf
Streifer, P. (2002). *Using data to make better educational decisions.* Lanham, MD: Scarecrow Education.
Streifer, P. (2004a, April). *A pilot study using artificial intelligence to determine key indicators to help improve student achievement.* Paper presented at the annual meeting of the American Educational Research Association, San Diego, CA.
Streifer, P. (2004b). *Tools & techniques for effective driven decision-making.* Lanham, MD: Scarecrow Education.
Thearling, K. (1997). *Understanding data mining: It's all in the interaction.* Retrieved January 7, 2003, from http://www.thearling.com/text/dsstar/interaction.htm
Two Crows Corporation. (1999). *Introduction to data mining and knowledge discovery* (3rd ed). Retrieved December 15, 2004, from http://www.twocrows.com/intro-dm.pdf

Involving Teachers in Data-Driven Decision Making: Using Computer Data Systems to Support Teacher Inquiry and Reflection

Jeffrey C. Wayman
Center for Social Organization of Schools
Johns Hopkins University

Accountability mandates such as No Child Left Behind (NCLB) have drawn attention to the practical use of student data for school improvement. Nevertheless, schools may struggle with these mandates because student data are often stored in forms that are difficult to access, manipulate, and interpret. Such access barriers additionally preclude the use of data at the classroom level to inform and impact instruction. Fortunately, there are newly available computer technologies that allow efficient organization and access to student data. In addition to allowing easier accountability reporting, these tools allow user-friendly data access at all educational levels, meaning that teachers can use these tools to engage in the informed reflection necessary to improve classroom practice. In this article, I discuss teacher use of these systems, providing insight into the function of these tools and discussing conditions that make these tools of the most service to teachers.

The use of data to inform educational decisions has recently drawn increased attention, spurred largely by accountability requirements set forth at the state and federal levels. A familiar example is the 2002 No Child Left Behind (NCLB) legislation, which mandates a significant increase in the gathering, aggregation, and upward reporting of student-level data. NCLB policy carries an implicit assumption that the availability of data will inform and initiate changes in teaching practice, but mechanisms for helping educators turn accountability data into actionable in-

---

Requests for reprints should be sent to Jeff Wayman, Center for Social Organization of Schools, Johns Hopkins University, 3003 N. Charles Street, Suite 200, Baltimore, MD 21218. E-mail: jwayman@csos.jhu.edu

formation are lacking in NCLB. Thus, although the NCLB legislation has provided much-needed stimulus for the gathering and presentation of student data at the school and district levels, it remains necessary to move beyond reporting mandates to provide teachers with the access and support needed to use these data in improving instruction.

State educational agencies, school districts, and other educational entities have collected and stored large amounts of student data for years. Despite this abundance, the employment of data to inform and improve educational practice has been the exception rather than the rule. In previous work, my colleagues and I have argued that one major barrier to the use of student data has been technical (Wayman, Stringfield, & Yakimowski, 2004): Although schools have been "data rich" for years, they were also "information poor" because the vast amounts of available data they had were often stored in ways that were inaccessible to most practitioners. Recently emerging technology is changing these circumstances. Computer tools have arrived on the market that provide fast, efficient organization and delivery of data. They also offer user-friendly interfaces that allow data analysis and presentation by all users, regardless of technological experience.

The new availability of these data systems not only helps expedite NCLB reporting at the school and district levels, but these systems also offer an additional, important feature. With classroom access to these tools, school systems have the opportunity to allow every teacher to have access to previously unattainable data describing their students. These data can be turned into information to improve classroom practice. Accompanied by the proper preparation and support, these tools provide schools with the efficient access necessary to reach beyond the basic requirements of NCLB and engage all educators in the rich application of student data to everyday classroom practice.

The data access provided by this technology is a necessary condition for informed inquiry into educational practice, but such access is not sufficient on its own. The mere presence of data does not automatically imply that usable information is available; educators need support to use these data to the fullest extent. Because the availability of these systems is relatively new, a large knowledge base describing best practices in applying these systems in the service of education does not yet exist. In this article, I provide a piece to this puzzle by describing conditions that best support the use of one form of these tools—data-warehousing and presentation systems.

SCHOOL DATA USE

The use of data to inform school practice may seem new because of the increased attention brought about by NCLB, but this concept has received varied attention in school research literature for more than 30 years. Many studies of positive outlier, "effective" schools demonstrating unusual gains in academic measures have shown that the thoughtful use of student data positively correlates with a range of measures of student achievement (e.g., Edmonds, 1979; Stringfield, 1994; Teddlie & Reynolds, 2000; Weber, 1971). Research on school improvement and school effectiveness has suggested that data use is central to the school improvement process (Chrispeels, 1992; Earl & Katz, 2002), and there are case studies available describing ways in which data has supported educational decisions (e.g., Feldman & Tung, 2001; Lachat, 2002; Pardini, 2000; Protheroe, 2001, Symonds, 2003).

Streifer (2002) listed exploring group differences, examining growth over time, program evaluation, and identifying root causes of educational problems as several ways data can be used. Chrispeels, Brown, and Castillo (2000) demonstrated that data use can be a strong predictor of the efficacy of school improvement teams: Data use not only increased efficacy directly but also served as a mediator for the positive effect of other factors. Chrispeels et al. described a longitudinal case study of a leadership team that saw the research role of this team evolve to be one of prominence over the 4 years of the study. Chrispeels and colleagues noted this as an empowering process: The more the team learned about and used data, the more data informed important decisions.

Case studies and interviews have suggested that data use may have a positive effect on the people involved in the educational process. Feldman and Tung (2001) observed that schools involved in data use often evolved toward a more professional culture. Educators in their study became more collaborative during the data/decision process, and school business consequently became less "privatized." Similarly, Nichols and Singer (2000) reported increased interdepartmental collaboration. One high school teacher in this study said, "We saw a total picture versus just our own department" (p. 36). Symonds (2003) presented a variety of data indicating that teachers involved in data inquiry were more collaborative. Earl and Katz (2002) noted that school leaders involved in data use often consider themselves in charge of their own destiny, increasingly able to find and use information to inform their school's improvement. Armstrong and Anthes (2001) and Massell (2001) found that data use was helpful in improving educator attitudes toward educational practice and students. Administrators in Massell's study viewed data use as stimulating a search for new ideas; data opportunities encouraged many to seek more professional development. Massell also found that increased communication and knowledge provided by data appeared to be positively altering educator attitudes toward the school capabilities of some underperforming groups. Armstrong and Anthes found the introduction of data use resulted in heightened teacher expectations of at-risk students, noting positive changes in teacher attitudes regarding the potential success of previously low-performing students.

Although accountability policies do not stress teacher involvement in data-based decision making, researchers such as Black and Wiliam (1998) have argued for a classroom-focused policy because of the access teachers have to students and their performance. Preliminary evidence suggests that, although they are often critical of accountability initiatives, teachers will embrace such policy when it is soundly implemented and responds to the learning needs of their students. Data presented by Ingram, Louis, and Schroeder (2004) and Massell (2001) showed that although teachers expressed concerns about the appropriateness of and importance assigned to assessments, they also recognized the new information afforded by assessments, along with the stimulus for new ideas brought about by inquiry. In short, research suggests that teachers are in favor of solutions that help improve the education of the children they teach.

We can paint a pleasant picture of the benefits of using data to inform school practice, but this picture must be moderated by findings from Stringfield, Reynolds, and Schaffer (2001): Many schools have found the thoughtful analysis of data to entail a great deal of labor, as data are often stored in ways that frustrate flexible analyses. In examining data use and observing schools, my colleagues and I have found this situation to be the rule rather than the exception. A positive response to this problem lies in the application of advanced computer technology to efficiently organize, store, and produce data for educator use (Wayman et al., 2004). The advent of educational data analysis tools represents a new opportunity to provide access to large amounts of student information that will facilitate more informed decision making and improve school performance. Such access should not be limited to administrative personnel: Teachers should also be involved. In the following section, we provide an introduction to data warehousing and reporting tools for this purpose.

AN INTRODUCTION TO DATA-WAREHOUSING AND PRESENTATION TOOLS

A burgeoning number of computer systems are being marketed for the purpose of efficiently delivering student data to educators, and these systems provide many different functions. Unfortunately, no system provides comprehensive access to solutions to educational problems, so districts must choose between many types of data systems. Common types of systems include (a) student information systems (SIS) that provide real-time accounting of daily school function (e.g., attendance, schedules) but are typically not designed to provide analysis or access to data beyond the current school year, (b) assessment systems that rapidly organize and analyze frequent benchmark assessments but are typically not designed to provide access to such data over time, and (c) data-warehousing systems that provide access to historic data of all types but are typically not designed for immediate turnaround of new data.

The types of functions available in today's computer systems are nearly mutually exclusive; that is, it is uncommon to find one type of system that incorporates the functionalities of another type of system. These lines are blurring; it is likely that technology will one day advance to the point where one system can perform all functions. Until then, school personnel need to choose the type of system that best fits their needs.

Although many types of data systems are useful for schools, I have chosen to focus on data-warehousing and presentation tools in this article. These systems offer unprecedented access to a wide range of historic data, with the capacity to retrieve a student's entire history for one analysis. Further, these tools provide user-friendly presentation interfaces that can provide data in an efficient, easily understood format and greatly reduce the amount of software training needed to use the system.

In education, the term *data warehousing* is often used to refer to the collection and organization of all data into one electronic repository. Data warehousing integrates data that are often stored in disconnected areas (e.g., student discipline data or achievement test data), thus allowing examination of relationships across a variety of domains. Although the concept may sound simple, organizing large, disparate databases into one common store is a complex task. Recent technological gains have resulted in tools and models that efficiently warehouse data for the examination of relationships commonly explored in the education arena. Data warehouse and presentation systems can be built using local talent or can be purchased commercially.

The data-warehousing process begins with an inventory of available data (if a district has contracted with a commercial vendor to implement a data system, the vendor usually offers help with the data inventory). After data identification is completed, school and/or vendor personnel begin the task of populating the data warehouse, often from a variety of locations and data systems (e.g., a student information system, Excel spreadsheets, paper records). Data warehouses serve as a common store of data but usually do not replace a school's other electronic data systems, such as the SIS. School personnel typically continue to maintain these systems for daily management and upload information from these systems into the data warehouse on a regular basis.

Once the data are available, user-friendly data presentation interfaces may be launched. These interfaces connect the user to the database and are the intermediaries through which users may examine relationships within the data. These systems typically offer the user two types of data access: preformatted reports or query tools.

Preformatted reports are previously compiled summaries of data that are available for viewing or printing with one click and require no specifications, alterations, or input from the user. For instance, a teacher might click on a link to view a report on students' achievement test scores, broken down by ethnicity and gender. Query tools allow ad hoc data specification, permitting the user to browse data or create customized reports. For instance, a teacher might use a query tool to explore achievement test histories of the students in a particular class, compose summaries of these histories based on desired groups, or simply browse available data.

In addition to unprecedented data access, these systems promise the ease of use that facilitates examination of student histories and learning tendencies. The data presentation interfaces offered by most commercial vendors are easy to learn and use, employing familiar Web-form elements such as check boxes and pull-down menus. Through these user-friendly systems, data are accessible to all educators of all levels of technical expertise. Most users who can check the weather or shop on the Internet can easily learn how to access student data using these interfaces.

COMMERCIALLY AVAILABLE DATA-WAREHOUSING AND PRESENTATION SOFTWARE

Many school districts have built their own data-warehousing and presentation systems for internal use. In addition, there are many commercially available systems for this purpose. Wayman et al. (2004) noted that because of specialization and efficiency, competent commercial vendors can usually get a system running in much less time than it would take to locally develop a system. In terms of both time and monetary costs, commercial systems may prove to be cheaper in the long term.

Should district personnel opt to buy a data-warehousing and presentation system, there are many commercially available systems from which to choose. Wayman et al. (2004) provided a report on data systems that offer access to existing student data. Along with issues surrounding implementation of such a system, this report also provided reviews of 13 software systems the authors identified as providing teacher-friendly access to student data. Updates to these reviews, along with other updated research on educational data-based decision making, are available at http://www.csos.jhu.edu/datause.

Commercially available programs for analyzing student data share several features that a school should expect when purchasing software for student-data management. For instance, most commercially available programs are Web-based and thus offer user access from any Internet connection. Additionally, these programs offer the capacity to produce reports based on the disaggregations mandated by the NCLB legislation, and all offer some form of ongoing technical support. Presently, however, there is no single system available that provides a full slate of features. Each system has strengths and weaknesses, so district personnel should take care to evaluate properly each system in terms of current and future needs.

Although the power and availability of these systems is exciting, their mere presence is probably not sufficient to fully support educators in turning data into actionable information. Unfortunately, little research has been conducted that examines best practices in encouraging widespread teacher use of these systems. In the following section, I offer three important areas that should be considered in providing support for the use of these tools.

SUPPORTING TEACHER USE OF STUDENT DATA SYSTEMS

Little evidence exists regarding best practices for involving entire teaching faculties in the examination of student data to improve classroom practice, especially using newly available technology. The current knowledge base on teacher use of student data is not typically based on the premise that every teacher should engage in data use to inform practice, nor have many studies been conducted in the presence of the widespread, easy data access described here. I advocate that these data systems be used to involve every teacher, not just a core group of interested parties. Further, data exploration with these systems should not become a burden. These systems should make a teacher's day better, not worse, and should help teachers to become more efficient practitioners. This situation presents a unique set of challenges.

In the following sections, I use prior research on data use to help inform suggestions for three important areas of support for teachers using these systems: professional development, leadership for a supportive data climate, and opportunities for collaboration.

Professional Development

Often, the analyses and inquiry employed to inform instructional improvement are not statistically complex (Herman & Gribbons, 2001; Streifer, 2002). In fact, usually there is a wealth of information available in simple descriptive statistics, easily provided by an adequate data system. The transformation of these data and summary statistics into practical, serviceable information is more difficult and requires proper training and professional development.

The lack of substantial and relevant professional development has been a barrier to many initiatives involving educational change (Newmann, King, & Youngs, 2000), and I anticipate this to be true of any data initiative. Listed by Armstrong and Anthes (2001) as a characteristic of a data-driven district, professional development is particularly crucial to the sustainability of a data initiative involving teachers and technology. Massell (2001) noted that most accountability policies implicitly assume that teachers understand how to turn data into information. Unfortunately, turning data into usable information is not an easy task. Further, most educators are not prepared to view their craft and their students' learning through the information lens (Herman & Gribbons, 2001; Massell, 2001), even in the presence of the type of data access described here.

Professional development for data use in schools is often implemented on a large scale and often without expectation of comprehensive teacher involvement, in spite of recommendations by a host of experts who have suggested that professional development and other forms of educator learning are better accomplished on a smaller, more personal scale (Schmoker, 2004). For example, Massell (2001) found that districts were likely to handle data instruction either through a central office that studies data and dispenses information to school personnel, or through the training of key personnel at each school, who are then responsible for handling the analyses and information for their school. Massell found that teachers were usually left to learn informally from other school personnel, rather than included in a professional development plan.

Large-scale professional development may not be an effective method to involve teachers in the use of new technology. Zhao and Frank (2003) suggested that successful technology implementation is not strongly impacted by large-scale professional development. In their study, teacher-to-teacher interaction had a strong positive impact on teacher use of technology, whereas training provided by the district did not. The authors asserted that the positive, informal help that teachers provide to each other—along with pressure to keep up—leads to the survival of a technology initiative.

Resources and guides for specific activities and topics to include in professional development for data use do exist (e.g., Bernhardt, 2004; Johnson, 2002; Wellman & Lipton, 2004). One practice that shows particular promise is the delivery of professional development and data support through an in-house expert, implemented in varied forms. Nichols and Singer (2000), for instance, described the use of "data mentors," where selected personnel from each school were trained in data techniques, then provided data analysis for teachers and helped support teachers in their own data use. Symonds (2003) advocated "classroom coaches" to support data use in addition to larger level professional development. Zhao and Frank (2003) described a situation in which teachers were allowed to learn on their own but were also encouraged to be part of a group that met regularly to help each other learn from data. In my own informal school observations, I have seen many situations in which a person on the school faculty became a de facto "go-to" person, serving as an unofficial "data facilitator" for both interpretation of data and the use of technology to deliver data.

The use of these tools must be augmented with relevant, ongoing professional development, regardless of the specific form chosen. Such support should be crafted with a careful eye to the unique situation presented when promoting widespread teacher involvement in data use.

Leadership for Supportive Data Climates

Successful implementation and teacher use of a data presentation system requires that the data initiative be supported by strong leadership. School leaders must not only model use of data but also establish conditions that support and encourage teachers to grow in their use of the system.

Fullan (1999) described the importance of strong leadership in any organizational initiative, and implementation of a successful data use initiative requires the same. Armstrong and Anthes (2001) and Massell (2001) both found that strong leadership and a supportive culture were characteristics of the schools in their studies that were most involved in data use. Symonds (2003) presented data that showed schools that were most proficient at closing the ethnic achievement gap were more likely to have school leaders who encouraged or led data-driven inquiry into the nature of the gap.

Leadership for inquiry through data use likely will involve a change in school culture and necessarily will involve teachers. In discussing the application of distributed leadership for inquiry, Copland (2003) noted that the structure for efficient inquiry must be allowed to evolve within the school context, with diverse individuals eventually assuming varied leadership roles. I believe that such an evolution will be particularly important in building teacher use of student data, given the frequent misalignment between teacher views and policy definitions of appropriate goals for student success. Ingram et al. (2004) found that teacher definitions of academic success were often more broadly defined than definitions set forth by accountability policy. Even in schools selected for exemplary improvement practices, teachers were found to rely heavily on anecdotal information in evaluating their students, often eschewing mandated assessments as merely necessary requirements.

The results from Ingram et al. (2004) highlight the importance of leadership to engage entire faculties in conversations to establish common goals and definitions concerning meaningful data. These results also highlight an important but often overlooked aspect of teaching culture: the importance placed by teachers on their own professional judgment. As professional educators, teachers rightly consider their judgment to be an important piece of knowledge, so they are likely to resist any initiative that ignores this judgment. Thus, it is important for school leaders to include teachers' professional judgment as a component of the information process—a data point, alongside such quantified data as assessments. As Black and Wiliam (1999) stated, "One strong reason for giving teachers a greater role is that they have access to the performance of their pupils in a variety of contexts and over extended periods of time" (p. 147).

Leadership support also includes allowing time for educators to immerse themselves in daily inquiry into their classroom practice (Armstrong & Anthes, 2001). Preliminary evidence suggests that teachers will embrace a properly supported data initiative when it is seen as an efficient way to improve education: Teachers in case studies often show quick enthusiasm for data when such data provide useful information for their classroom practice (Symonds, 2003), and data initiatives that stimulate a search for new ideas are seen as most successful for busy educators (Earl & Katz, 2002; Feldman & Tung, 2001; Massell, 2001). Regardless of the efficiency benefits of the time-saving data tools described here, time demands on teachers are heavy, so teachers may participate more fully in a data initiative when they are provided time to do so. The same holds true when incorporating technology into an initiative. Zhao and Frank (2003) noted the importance of offering time to explore newly implemented technology and summarized research showing that teachers are more likely to use a particular technology if it is supportive of their teaching tasks and does not require a great deal of additional personal investment.

Collaboration

The data systems described here present two new issues for most teachers: using software to organize data and using data to produce information. Initial start-up training on both fronts is important, but beyond that, I believe that teachers will best progress as reflective practitioners through various forms of collaboration with other educators.

Collaboration and information sharing is a common theme in educational improvement. For example, Schmoker (2004) cited a large group of prominent researchers in arguing that improvement of the teaching craft is not attained through the isolationism that marks most schools but by frequent discussion and activities centered around teaching practice. Organizational strategists like Fullan (Fullan, 1999; Fullan & Miles, 1992) have noted that incorporating diverse ideas and perspectives is important to the health of any system. Understandably, professional collaboration is easier to implement when a common theme or vision exists; data offer a viable topic because of data's relevance to all involved. Combining a data initiative with professional collaboration not only offers the opportunity for teachers to learn the art of data use from each other but also allows for a fertile exchange of ideas and strategies.

Case studies on data use suggest the relationship between data use and collaboration is a reciprocal one: Data initiatives are more likely to be successful if teachers are allowed to learn and work collaboratively, and the use of data helps foster constructive collaboration (Chrispeels et al., 2000; Feldman & Tung, 2001; Nichols & Singer, 2000; Symonds, 2003). Symonds (2003) reported that teachers using data in schools that achieved a decrease in ethnic achievement gaps discussed data more with colleagues, visited colleagues' classrooms more, and had more general instances of collaboration. The author and the teachers in the study advocated strongly for collaboration as an avenue to enhance the effectiveness of data use. Collaboration should also be a positive force in increasing interest in the data technology endorsed here, along with the technical skills for using these tools. Zhao and Frank (2003) found their teacher interaction construct to be a prominent factor in teacher use of technology, stating that the survival of any technology initiative depends on a school's social relations. Zhao and Frank also suggested that positive teacher interaction is crucial to the survival of an initiative.

Collaboration resulting from data use can benefit teaching faculties beyond one-to-one relationships. Nichols and Singer (2000) reported increased interdepartmental collaboration as a result of data initiatives, citing one teacher who touted the increased understanding these collaborations fostered. Massell (2001) saw more interschool and interdistrict communication as a result of data use, providing examples of districts that paired low-performing and high-performing schools based on the similarity of their data, and schools that sought out other schools with similar data profiles to explore best practices. In these examples, data formed the common ground on which these educators could meet and adapt strategies from others in similar contexts. Copland (2003) described the process of inquiry with the framework of a "distributed leadership" culture, in which responsibilities for inquiry into the improvement of teaching and learning were shared by administrators and teachers. These studies illustrate that using data within a collaborative framework not only affords teachers more opportunities not only to interact and share ideas but also to interact with and assume a variety of roles in the educational hierarchy.

Although much collaboration will happen as a result of a data-use initiative, it is also wise to establish structures for collaborative data use and to preserve these data tools as main ingredients of collaboration. Examples of these include a form of distributed leadership (Copland, 2003), schoolwide data workgroups, and data committees that support individual data exploration. Although widely advocated, collaboration can be difficult to implement. Gunn and King (2003) pointed out that inattention to school cultural issues, like implicit power relationships, can quickly undermine collaborative work. They also suggested that many pitfalls could be avoided by engaging in substantive discussions of teaching and learning, establishing a collective understanding of goals, and engaging in professional staff inquiry.

CONCLUSION

As Earl and Katz (2002) noted, the use of data for school improvement is no longer a choice; it is a must. Turning data into actionable information is a multifaceted process, and the supporting research base is still young. In this article, I have addressed one component of this process: the use of data-warehousing and presentation tools to help teachers efficiently become more informed, reflective practitioners.

Accountability measures such as NCLB provide for evaluations of districts and schools and have served to bring attention to the large amount of student data available for use. It is also important that schools look beyond NCLB requirements to move student data into the hands of teachers. The software systems described here provide an effective mechanism for this purpose. Whether locally developed or commercially purchased, these tools bring an efficiency and stability to the data process that has been lacking for years. It is my position that without such tools, districts not only may have difficulty meeting minimum reporting requirements but also will likely be unable to dig more deeply into their data and become immersed in the inquiry process.

The prospect of implementing a data-warehouse and reporting system can be an exciting one for many schools and districts. Such a system can provide the spark for a systemwide change in thinking and practice that often comes when a school begins to view student learning through the data lens. These systems are also applicable to any educational context. And although it is true that the implementation of these systems demands a financial investment, this investment can be very cost-effective when one accounts for the potential improvement in teacher practice and student learning.

Much research is needed on the use of these powerful tools. In this article, I have speculated on best practices in the use of these systems, based on research in other settings. Although useful, research in other settings is no substitute for research in this setting, especially in light of the growing popularity of these systems. As school systems move to buy and implement these systems, it is necessary to properly identify conditions in which these tools can be used to best support the conduct of education. Armed with this knowledge, rigorous, controlled studies can then be conducted to describe the degree of value added to the educational experience by different applications and implementations of these systems. I hope to join with other researchers in providing these important pieces to the research puzzle and helping to move these data systems from exciting possibilities to beneficial, invaluable educational tools.

ACKNOWLEDGMENTS

The work reported herein was supported under the Center for Research on the Education of Students Placed At Risk (CRESPAR), PR/Award No. OERI-R–117-D40005, as administered by the Institute of Education Sciences (IES), U.S. Department of Education (USDoE). The contents, findings and opinions expressed here are those of the author and do not necessarily represent the positions or policies of the National Institute on the Education of At-Risk Students, IES, or the USDoE.

REFERENCES

Armstrong, J., & Anthes, K. (2001). How data can help. *American School Board Journal 188*(11), 38–41.
Bernhardt, V. (2004). *Data analysis for continuous school improvement.* Larchmont, NY: Eye on Education.
Black, P., & Wiliam, D. (1998). Inside the black box: Raising standards through student assessment. *Phi Delta Kappan, 80,* 139–148.
Chrispeels, J. H. (1992). *Purposeful restructuring: Creating a climate of learning and achievement in elementary schools.* London: Falmer.
Chrispeels, J. H., Brown, J. H., & Castillo, S. (2000). School leadership teams: Factors that influence their development and effectiveness. *Advances in Research and Theories of School Management and Educational Policy, 4,* 39–73.
Copland, M. A. (2003). Leadership of inquiry: Building and sustaining capacity for school improvement. *Educational Evaluation and Policy Analysis, 25,* 375–395.
Earl, L., & Katz, S. (2002). Leading schools in a data-rich world. In K. Leithwood & P. Hallinger (Eds.), *Second international handbook of educational leadership and administration* (pp. 1003–1022). Dordrecht, Netherlands: Kluwer Academic.
Edmonds, R. (1979). Effective schools for the urban poor. *Educational Leadership, 37*(1), 15–27.
Feldman, J., & Tung, R. (2001). Using data-based inquiry and decision making to improve instruction. *ERS Spectrum 19*(3), 10–19.
Fullan, M. (1999). *Change forces: The sequel.* London: Falmer.
Fullan, M. G., & Miles, M. M. (1992). Getting reform right: What works and what doesn't. *Phi Delta Kappan, 73,* 744–752.
Gunn, J. H., & King, B. (2003). Trouble in paradise: Power, conflict, and community in an interdisciplinary teaching team. *Urban Education, 38,* 173–195.
Herman, J. L., & Gribbons, B. (2001). *Lessons learned in using data to support school inquiry and continuous improvement: Final report to the Stuart Foundation* (CSE Tech. Rep. No. 535). Los Angeles: University of California, Center for the Study of Evaluation.
Ingram, D., Louis, K. S., & Schroeder, R. G. (2004). Accountability policies and teacher decision making: Barriers to the use of data to improve practice. *Teachers College Record, 106,* 1258–1287.
Johnson, R. (2002). *Using data to close the achievement gap: How to measure equity in our schools* (1st ed.). Thousand Oaks, CA: Corwin.
Lachat, M.A. (2002). *Data-driven high school reform: The breaking ranks model.* Hampton, NH: Center for Resource Management.
Massell, D. (2001). The theory and practice of using data to build capacity: State and local strategies and their effects. In S. H. Fuhrman (Ed.), *From the capitol to the classroom: Standards-based reform in the states* (pp. 148–169). Chicago: University of Chicago Press.
Newmann, F., King, B., & Youngs, P. (2000). Professional development that addresses school capacity: Lessons from urban elementary schools. *American Journal of Education, 108,* 259–299.
Nichols, B. W., & Singer, K. P. (2000). Developing data mentors. *Educational Leadership, 57*(5), 34–37.
Pardini, P. (2000). Data, well done. *Journal of Staff Development 21*(1), 12–18.
Protheroe, N. (2001). Improving teaching and learning with data-based decisions: Asking the right questions and acting on the answers. *ERS Spectrum 19*(3), 4–9.
Streifer, P. A. (2002). *Using data to make better educational decisions.* Lanham, MD: Scarecrow Press.
Stringfield, S. (1994). Outlier studies of school effects. In D. Reynolds, B. Creemers, P. Nesselrodt, E. Schaffer, S. Stringfield, & C. Teddlie (Eds.), *Advances in school effectiveness research* (pp. 73–83). Oxford, England: Pergamon.

Stringfield, S., Reynolds, D., & Schaffer, E. (2001, January). *Fifth-year results from the High Reliability Schools project.* Symposium presented at the meeting of the International Congress for School Effectiveness and Improvement, Toronto, Canada.

Schmoker, M. (2004). Tipping point: From feckless reform to substantive instructional improvement. *Phi Delta Kappan, 85,* 424–432.

Symonds, K. W. (2003). *After the test: How schools are using data to close the achievement gap.* San Francisco: Bay Area School Reform Collaborative.

Teddlie, C., & Reynolds, D. (2000). *The international handbook of school effectiveness research.* London: Falmer.

Wayman, J. C., Stringfield, S., & Yakimowski, M. (2004). *Software enabling school improvement through the analysis of student data* (Report No. 67). Retrieved December 14, 2004, from Center for Social Organization of Schools Web site: http://www.csos.jhu.edu/crespar/techReports/Report 67.pdf

Weber, G. (1971). *Inner city children can be taught to read: Four successful schools* (Occasional Paper No. 18). Washington, DC: Council for Basic Education.

Wellman, B., & Lipton, L. (2004). *Data-driven dialogue: A facilitator's guide to collaborative inquiry.* Sherman, CT: MiraVia.

Zhao, Y., & Frank, K. A. (2003). Factors affecting technology users in schools: An ecological perspective. *American Educational Research Journal, 40,* 807–840.

Identifying and Monitoring Students' Learning Needs With Technology

Eva Chen, Margaret Heritage, and John Lee
National Center for Research on Evaluation, Standards, and Student Testing (CRESST)
University of California, Los Angeles

This article presents initial findings from an evaluation research study of the implementation of a Web-based decision support tool, the Quality School Portfolio (QSP), developed at the National Center for Research on Evaluation, Standards, and Student Testing (CRESST) at the University of California, Los Angeles (UCLA). The study focused on users' experiences with the training for and implementation of QSP. Data were collected by telephone interviews. The results show that QSP provided educators with enhanced access to more extensive and broadly founded student data and with the ability to analyze student data to identify at-risk students. Additionally, QSP was found to promote collaboration and shared planning among educators. It is concluded that technology tools, which can facilitate the analysis and reporting of educational data, have opened up the prospect of timely identification of at-risk students and interventions to meet their educational needs. Tools like this also support sound assessment practices, providing opportunities for frequent assessment and other evidence of competency beyond standardized testing.

At the end of the 19th century, John Dewey (1897) wrote, "Education must begin with an insight into the child's capacities, interests, and habits. It must be controlled at every point by reference to these same considerations. ... These powers, interests, and habits must be continually interpreted—we must know what they mean" (p. 2). Additionally, he went on to say, "I believe that all questions of the grading of the child and his promotion should be determined by reference to the same standard" (p. 2). In 2001, the No Child Left Behind Act (NCLB) established provisions for "annual testing in every grade" to give teachers "the information

---

Requests for reprints should be sent to Eva Chen, CRESST/UCLA, 300 Charles E. Young Drive North, GSE&IS Bldg. 3rd Fl./Mailbox 951522, Los Angeles, CA 90095-1522. E-mail: echen@cse.ucla.edu

they need to ensure that every child will reach academic success." Although written 104 years apart, these two messages exhibit similarities: Educators need information about children's progress and development to plan their learning, and they must evaluate that progress by reference to common standards.

However, there have been significant changes that set Dewey's time apart from the present day. We know much more about how to assess students' "capacities, interests, and habits." We have much more evidence about what happens to students when we fail to pay close attention to their learning and the difficulties they may be experiencing. And we have technology that can help educators assess and monitor how their students' learning is progressing, permitting ongoing formative, as well as summative, evaluation.

In this article, we provide a perspective on how educators can use technology to assist them in assessing and identifying low-performing students and in planning interventions to meet their needs. Specifically, we describe a pilot implementation study of a technology tool, the Quality School Portfolio (QSP), and initial findings on its impact on educators' practices related to the identification of students' learning needs.

RESEARCH CONTEXT

Monitoring Students' Needs

Although there are similarities between the messages of Dewey and NCLB, there are very significant differences between the two. NCLB refers to annual testing as a means to academic success, defined as meeting established state standards, whereas Dewey referred to continual interpretation of "powers, interests, and habits." Although annual tests are intended as a lever to improve student performance, a number of factors limit their effectiveness as a tool for improving student achievement. Paramount among these factors is the frequency with which these tests are administered (Baker, 2001; Herman & Gribbons, 2001; Shepard, 2004). Infrequent administration of assessments unavoidably yields results reflecting aspects of learning at a coarse-grained level, which do not give information about the detailed nature of student learning needed by school teachers to guide instructional planning. Annual tests tell teachers how well students did on the test, but they give limited information about what students did well on, and even less information about why they did well (Smithson & Porter, 2004). Moreover, "one assessment does not fit all" (National Research Council [NRC], 2001, p. 220), and the validity of inferences drawn from a measure depends on the purpose for which that measure is intended (American Educational Research Association [AERA], 2000; AERA, American Psychological Association, & National Council on Measurement in Education, 1999).

In contrast to NCLB, Dewey suggested "continual interpretation," which necessarily requires much more frequent and fine-grained assessments linked to the goals of teachers in the classroom. These assessments can provide evidence that can be used "to adapt the teaching work to meet the learning needs" (Black & Wiliam, 2004, p. 22).

Dewey also took a broader perspective than NCLB about what educators need to focus their attention on. In addition to children's capacities, he included habits and interests as components of development. Information about students' habits and interests can help teachers adapt the curriculum and select instructional strategies that both respond to and support the development of students' interests and ways of learning.

Additionally, recent work has stressed the importance of information from sources other than measures of academic achievement to examine the factors that contribute to student performance. Understanding the context of student achievement can be just as central to improved achievement as knowing the parameters of test performance (Baker, Linn, Herman, & Koretz, 2002).

Closing the Achievement Gap

The central goal of NCLB is closing the achievement gap. Annual reporting of the performance of subgroups of students is mandated to ensure that all groups of students are making progress. But reporting annual test scores alone will not make the difference for groups of students who lag behind their peers and are not meeting the standards. What is needed, as Dewey exhorted, is continual monitoring and interpretation of performance so that students who risk not meeting standards can be identified early and steps can be taken to provide additional support.

When at-risk students are identified early, they can make significant gains in achievement. For example, there is a wealth of evidence that shows the positive impact of early intervention for very young children (Berrueta-Clement, Schweinhart, Barnett, Epstein, & Weikart, 1984; Bryant & Maxwell, 1997; Campbell & Ramey, 1995; Garber, 1988; Jester & Guinagh, 1983; Johnson & Walker, 1991; Lally, Mangione, & Honig, 1988). In testimony to the House Education Committee, Reid Lyon, chief of the Development and Behavior Branch, National Institute of Child Health and Human Development, National Institutes of Health, reported that "there is evidence that if children receive effective instruction early and intensively, they can often make large gains in academic achievement" and that "we have scientific evidence that early intervention can greatly reduce the number of older children who are identified as [learning disabled]" (Lyon, 2002). Indeed, data derived from the U.S. Department of Education, Office of Special Education Programs (OSEP) show that 60% of children served under the Individuals with Disabilities Act are identified too late to benefit from effective interventions

(U.S. Department of Education, 2001). Thus, identifying and providing support for at-risk students will be essential to efforts to close the achievement gap.

Although annual test scores, as mandated by NCLB, can highlight program strengths and weaknesses, and an item analysis (if it is provided to teachers) can help identify specific areas in which students are experiencing difficulties, more frequent diagnostic assessments can play a significant role in identifying areas of difficulty for at-risk students. Once difficulties have been clearly identified, teachers will have detailed information to plan instruction in response to specific student needs, and continuous monitoring of student performance will assist teachers in adapting their teaching to ensure successful learning.

New Help for Educators

To a great degree, successful use of data to meet students' needs is dependent on districts' and schools' data-storage and -access capacity. However, educational institutions traditionally lack the capacity to store, retrieve, integrate, and analyze data (Cizek, 2000; Holcomb, 1999; Wise, Lukin, & Roos, 1991).

Tools are increasingly available that enable educators to store information and analyze data (see, e.g., Wayman, Stringfield, & Yakimowski, 2004). One tool of this kind is the QSP, developed at the National Center for Research on Evaluation, Standards, and Student Testing (CRESST) at the University of California, Los Angeles (UCLA), with funding from the U.S. Department of Education. QSP is designed to assist schools and districts in meeting the reporting requirements of the NCLB and to improve educators' ability to use information that will help meet the needs of those students who are at risk of not meeting standards.

NCLB requires annual reporting of achievement levels on statewide tests disaggregated by six subgroups. However, given the limitations of these tests for teachers to identify and monitor individuals' needs, and recalling Dewey's statement about interpreting the child's interests and habits, QSP gives administrators and teachers the capability to include a wide range of achievement and other kinds of data, in addition to the state test data. Thus, educators have access to multiple measures of performance, both formative and summative, and to other measures related to students' learning.

QSP permits analysis of all types of data. When used for the analysis of multiple measures, descriptive data are valuable for identifying students' needs. In addition to descriptive analysis, QSP users can conduct comparative and correlation analyses. Comparison analysis can be used to examine the performance of student groups in ways that go beyond describing the current status of their achievement, and correlation analysis can be used to examine the factors that may be related to student learning.

Core features of QSP are the longitudinal student database, disaggregation capabilities, report functions, goals and monitoring functions, a gradebook, and a digital portfolio. Color-coded tabs organize all of the QSP functions, akin to a filing system. Next, we present a description of each tab and the ways in which the program's functions can be used to identify at-risk students.

Students tab. Using QSP, educators can create an individual, longitudinal record for each student, including demographic information and assessment information (e.g., from annual tests, diagnostic tests, classroom-based assessments). The record can also include data related to students' perceptions, interests, habits, and opportunities to learn (OTL). For example, demographic information can include a student's age, ethnicity, and language spoken at home. Assessment information can include data from annual statewide tests; because QSP can be customized to meet site-specific needs, district- and classroom-based assessments can also be included. Information on students, teachers, and parents from surveys, interviews, and observations about other aspects of students' learning (e.g., motivation, particular interests, OTL) can be added. With the Students tab, administrators and teachers can have easy access to each student's history to identify persistent problems and monitor progress over time. Figure 1 depicts the Student History subtab of the Students tab with individual student results over time.

Groups tab. Test and other data can be disaggregated by various groups in the Groups tab. Users can create three types of groups: system, custom, and combination. System groups, which represent the first level of disaggregation (e.g., male and female), are automatically created in the system. Custom groups are created based on students' performance on various measures, including state, district, and classroom assessments (e.g., students scoring at the bottom quartile in math, represented as norm reference test [NRT] Math ≤ 25). Additionally, users can combine system and custom groups together to make a combination group. For example, teachers wanting to identify low-performing students on a number of measures could create one or more combination groups. First, they would create custom groups for each measure consisting of the lowest performing students (e.g., NRT Math ≤ 25, NRT Language Arts ≤ 25, District Reading $\leq$ Below Basic, performance based assessment (PBA) Math ≤ 2, etc.). Next, they would combine the custom groups and, at that point, QSP would locate the students who meet the criteria. The teachers would then be able to see a list of the individual students who comprise the low-performing combination group.

Using the disaggregation capability in the Groups tab, educators can reveal hidden patterns in the data. For example, in a school with a high average score, it may be that subgroups of students (including those in the at-risk group) are not doing well, but their poorer performance is hidden because the higher performing students' scores are masking those of the subgroups.

The Groups function can also assist in program evaluation. In a situation in which administrators want to determine the effectiveness of an intervention pro-

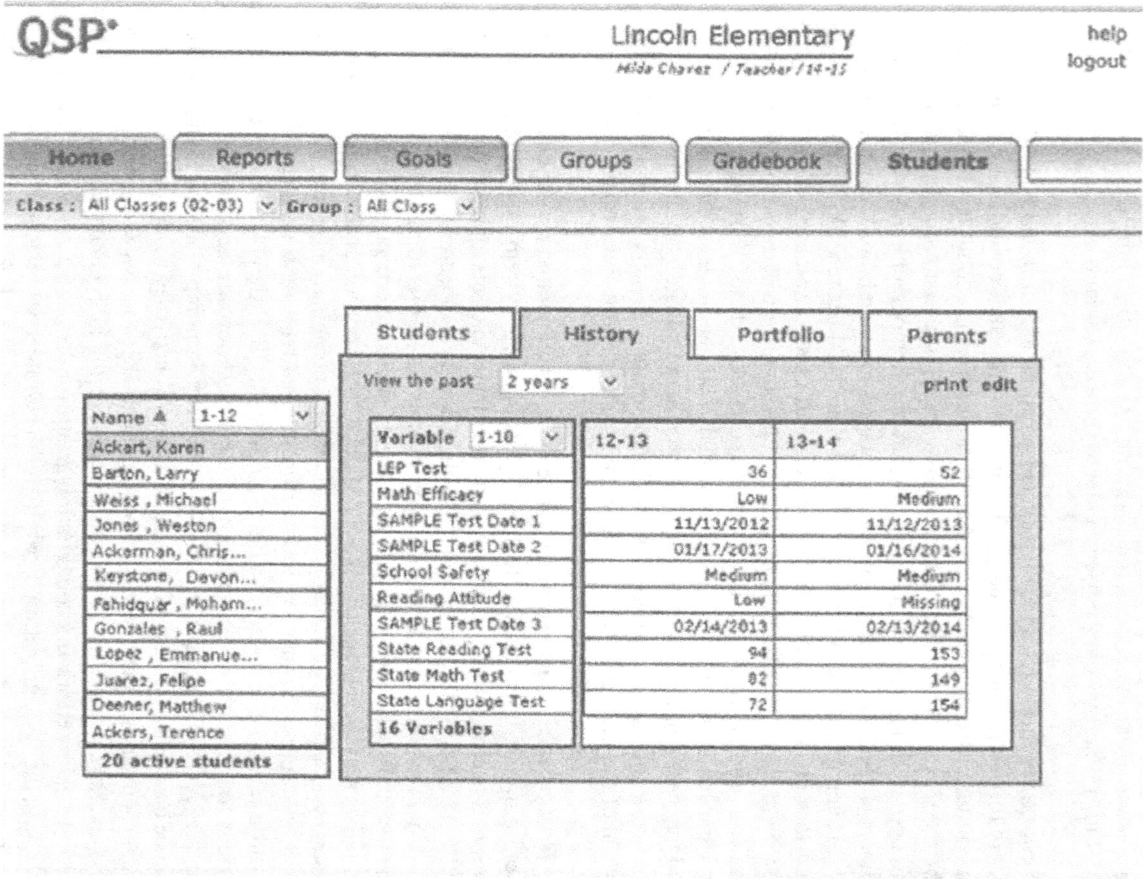

FIGURE 1 Student History subtab of the Students tab showing individual student results for prior years.

gram, they could construct the variable *participation in the program* and generate groups according to this variable. The performance of these students, pre- and post-intervention, could be compared. Additionally, a comparison of their performance to those students who had not received the intervention could be made.

Reports tab. Once the groups have been defined in the Groups tab, easily understandable reports can be generated to display the performance of the groups. QSP has 23 reporting options, and users can select the most appropriate report for the analysis they are conducting. In the previously cited example of the combination group of low-performing students, a pie chart could identify the ethnic composition of the group; a cohort line graph could show the group's performance in previous years.

To investigate the factors that may be impacting the performance of these students, educators could use data about students' perceptions of school or their motivation levels in conjunction with the achievement data. For example, a floating bar chart could be created for the low-performing group, with each bar representing the level of motivation (with motivation categorized in the system as low, medium, and high). Educators could see if motivation level was a factor that could be impacting reading scores.

In addition, in the Reports tab, teachers can quickly and easily create individualized student progress reports that show the up-to-the-minute status of students' performance on a range of classroom measures. The progress reports can be printed and sent home, or parents can be invited to view the progress reports online. In this way, parents are continuously informed about their child's progress, and they have the opportunity to be involved in their child's learning, which is especially important if the child is experiencing difficulties. Figure 2 shows some of the reporting options in QSP.

Goals tab. Using the Goals function, educators can determine achievement goals and set targets that need to be met for the goal to be attained. The targets for each goal to be met are identified and specified as mandatory or optional. An example of a mandatory target might be as follows: 100% of the at-risk students will perform at ≥ 60 on the districtwide reading test. An optional target might be: 100% of these same students will perform at the proficient level on the schoolwide reading test. Once goals and targets are established, strategies for meeting them can be identified and documented in QSP. The process of documentation permits school personnel to keep a record of the effectiveness of the strategies for particular targets.

QSP enables administrators and teachers to closely monitor students' progress toward meeting the goal through a report, which is a timeline-based representation of the targets and can show which targets have been met and which have not. In ad-

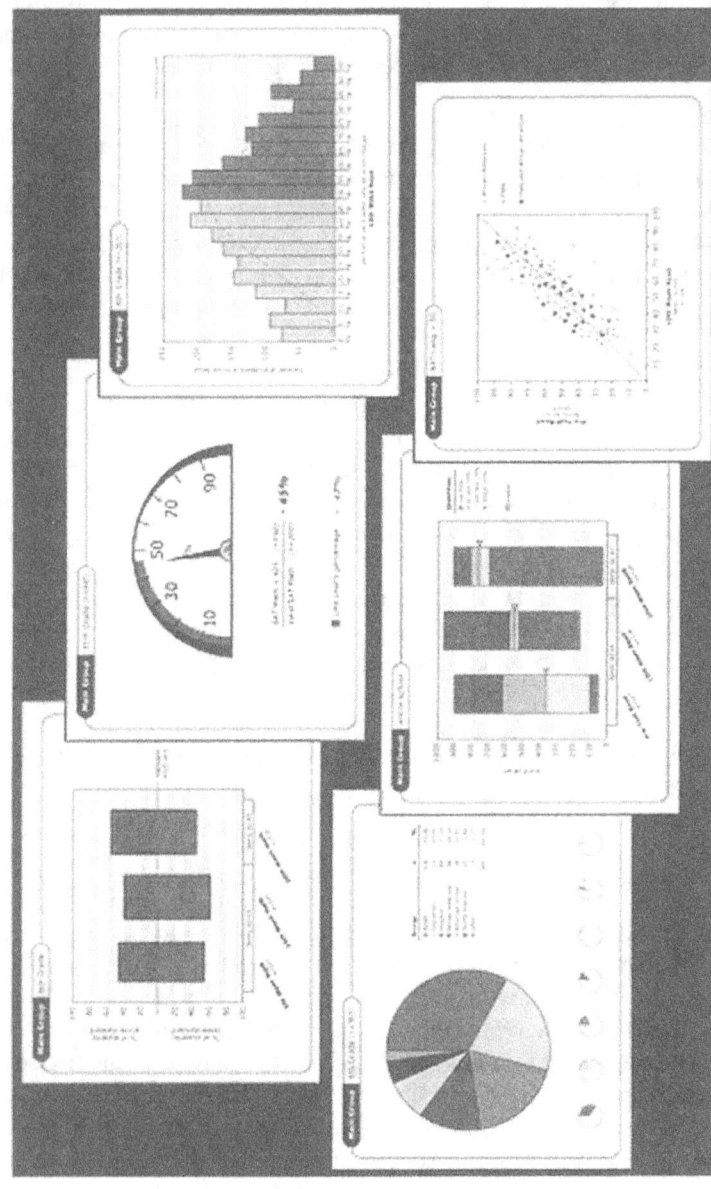

FIGURE 2 Example report options (out of 23): floating bar chart, gauge, histogram, pie chart, multilevel floating bar chart, and scatterplot.

dition, using the "view +" and "view –" features, they can select a target and see those students who are meeting the target and those who are not.

Gradebook. There are two forms of gradebook in QSP. One functions like a traditional gradebook and permits percentage and letter-based grading. The other is a standards-based gradebook in which the teacher connects standards with assessments and rates the students' progress with reference to the standards. A distinctive feature of the QSP gradebook is that it links to a digital portfolio in which other performance data can be stored.

Digital portfolio. Samples of student work and performance can be stored in the digital portfolio in a range of media, including text, image, video, and audio. For example, teachers could store video or audio samples of their students reading aloud followed by a retelling of what they had read. To determine the specific difficulties of low-achieving students, they could turn to the examples in the portfolio for detailed information about how the students were reading over a period of time. In a similar way, teachers can derive more detailed information about writing performance over time by examining writing samples stored in the portfolio. Portfolio items can be easily shared among colleagues so that teachers in one content area can see students' achievement in other areas of the curriculum. The portfolio can be used as a tool both to identify specific needs and to monitor progress. Figure 3 depicts the Portfolio subtab of the Students tab with a link to a video sample of student reading.

Preparing, Importing, and Maintaining Data in QSP

Any data-analysis and -reporting tool will be only as good as the quality and quantity of the data that goes into it. QSP is no exception. As a first step in obtaining quality data, Wayman et al. (2004) emphasized that schools and districts need to thoroughly assess their data, data needs, and available resources; they also must ensure that their data are clean. This includes taking a data inventory, surveying analysis needs, and determining whether to implement the system using local staff or external contractors.

From a data inventory, schools and districts can determine where the data are located and, based on an analysis of data needs, decide (a) what existing data they have to meet the analysis needs and (b) what additional data they will need to collect. Ultimately, the richer the data set, the more potential there is for worthwhile analysis.

Before the data are imported into QSP, there are several issues that need to be addressed. First, in QSP, data elements are categorized as numeric, categorical, permanent, or changing; date formats are also used. It is essential for information technology (IT) personnel and decision makers to agree on how the data will be

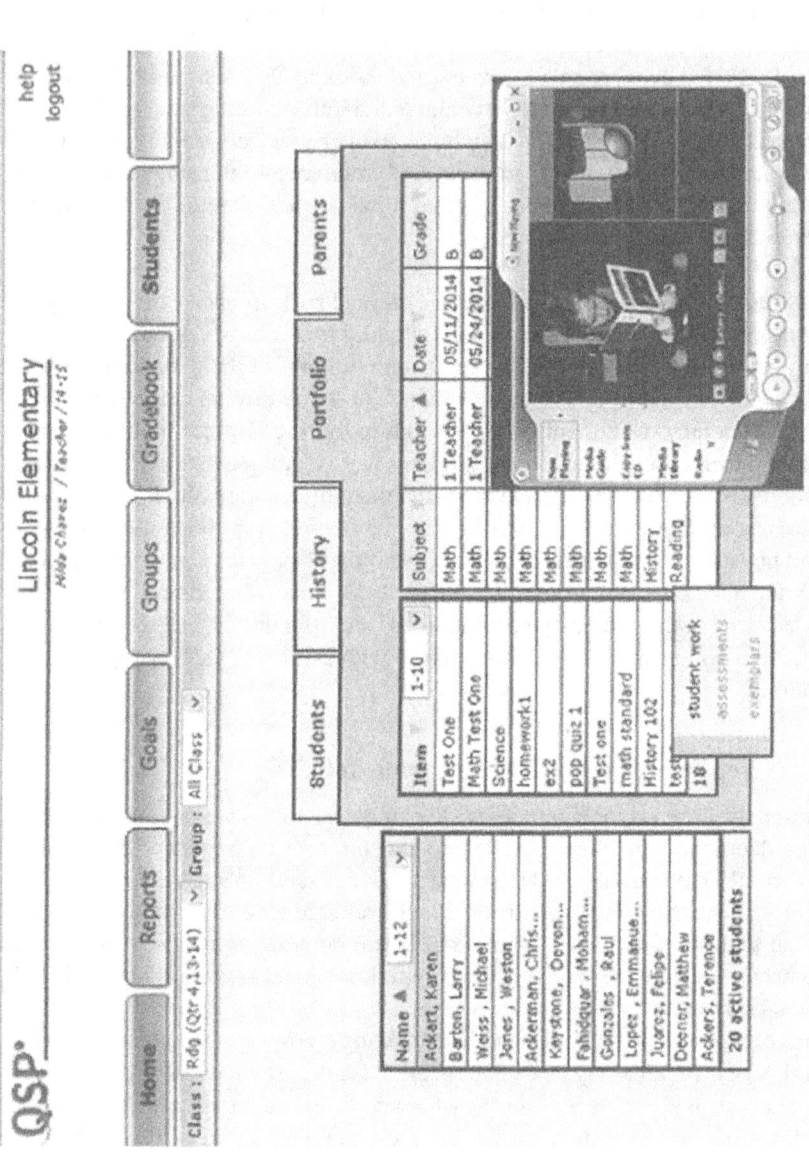

FIGURE 3   Digital portfolio including a link to a sample video of a student's work.

categorized in the system. For those districts that share one server within a consortium arrangement, it is particularly important to standardize how data are coded.

The second issue is data cleaning. QSP requires unique student identification numbers (IDs). However, in many schools and districts, data files have missing IDs or do not have unique student IDs. There are moves afoot in many states to create new state-level unique IDs, which will need to be matched in the system to any existing IDs to ensure the integrity of the data and to enable historical data to be maintained consistently. Although some schools and districts have relatively clean data, our experience of QSP implementation has suggested that an allocation of considerable time and effort will be required by most schools and school systems across the country to make sure that the data are useful and accurate.

Third, testing companies will often provide data in one long text file, with a codebook describing which data are in which field positions. To be brought into QSP, these files need to be converted into comma-separated values files. QSP has a universal parser that does this conversion.

Once the data are prepared, they can be imported into QSP in one of three ways. At the system-administrator level, data are imported via a Web-based wizard; in the case of large files, imports are made via a personal computer (PC) tool. Data can also be imported by classroom teachers; teachers can enter classroom-level data into the gradebook and link or upload items to be stored in the digital portfolio.

Currently, QSP is undergoing changes that will enable the database to be updated through Schools Interoperability Framework (SIF) variables. SIF, instituted in 1997, is a growing set of data-exchange standards that facilitate communication among software applications that are being developed by a collaboration of school-data stakeholders.[1] The importation of data into QSP will become easier as more systems become SIF-compliant. The need to enter or import data in multiple systems will be reduced, and the speed of updating information will increase.

A further consideration in QSP implementation is identifying who will be responsible for cleaning and importing the data and keeping accurate and up-to-date data. Our experience with QSP has shown the benefit of having technical personnel who have expertise in database maintenance as well as in data preparation and cleaning. For those districts that lack technical expertise in data and database management, these tasks can be outsourced to external agencies. Wayman et al. (2004) stressed the importance of rapid, successful implementation of data tools for the long-term development of a data-based decision-making climate. Districts that do not have sufficient in-house resources to ensure successful implementation could outsource data cleaning and data management.

---

[1] See http://www.sifinfo.org/index.asp

QSP Rollout

A national rollout of QSP began in early February 2003. To support the rollout, CRESST provided training for IT personnel and decision makers, particularly administrators and teachers. IT personnel received training in setting up the server, installing the software, and importing data. The decision makers' training focused on data-use skills.

The multiple uses of QSP described earlier assume that users have the skills needed to use data. However, in reality, educators often lack the skills to make effective use of data (Baker, 2003; Choppin, 2002; Cizek, 2000). Traditionally, neither administrators nor teachers receive formal training in how to assess students or make use of assessment information. As Stiggins (2002) noted, U.S. educators remain "a national faculty unschooled in the principles of sound assessment" (p. 5). Moreover, professional preparation rarely includes training in the data-analysis skills needed to use data to improve student achievement (Cromey, 2000).

The CRESST training program was designed to help practitioners acquire effective data use skills. The program comprises five online, self-paced, interactive modules. In addition to offering training in how to use the software, the CRESST training program focuses on a process and five core skills to use data effectively. Figure 4

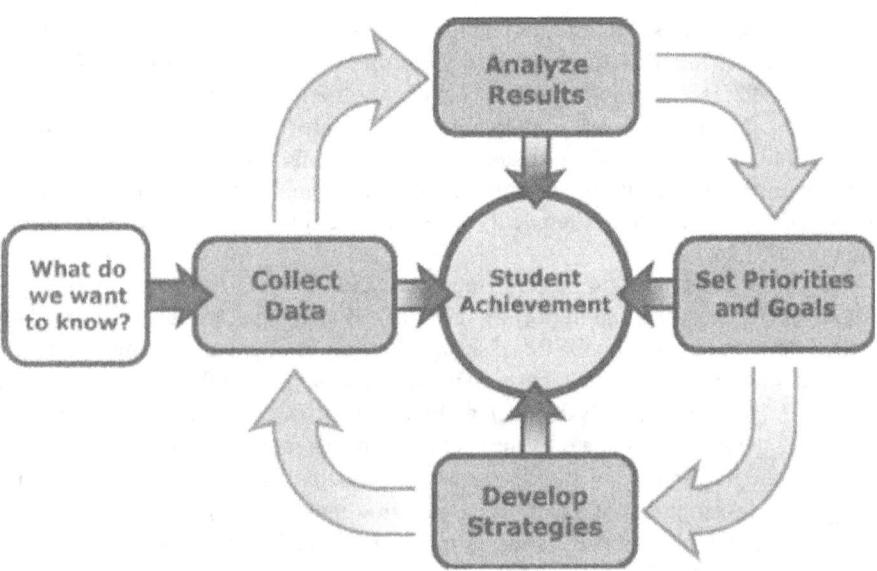

FIGURE 4 Process for investigating data to identify students' needs.

shows the cyclical process used in the training for investigating data to identify students' needs.

This process involves asking questions, collecting data, analyzing and interpreting data, and setting goals, targets, and strategies for each priority area. Embedded in each component of the cycle are essential data-use skills. These include skills in designing well-framed questions for data analysis; collecting quality data that can contribute to an understanding of students' needs (including determining the reliability and validity of data); understanding the types of data analysis; establishing clear goals for students' learning; and devising strategies to meet and monitor the goals.

QSP Implementation Evaluation

Simultaneous to the QSP rollout, an evaluation research study was conducted from Spring 2003 to Fall 2004 to investigate how schools and districts implemented QSP and how QSP affected data use and decision making for improving student achievement. Phone interviews were conducted with 33 educators from 22 districts in 12 states across the country who had been using QSP for several months. The interview asked the participants to comment on their experiences using QSP; their goals in using this assessment tool; the effectiveness of the training sessions; the support they received at the school and district level for QSP implementation; the ways in which they used QSP to collect, store, and analyze student performance and background data; and the ways in which QSP affected their data access and data use for making decisions to improve students' learning.

Qualitative data analysis was conducted and all the interview tapes were transcribed and coded to examine patterns and themes illustrating implementation, users' experience with QSP, and perceived impact of QSP on data use and student achievement. Coded data were examined to compare different patterns of QSP implementation across different districts. The interview data showed that QSP implementation had an initial impact on (a) enhancing school data access, (b) identifying students' needs in learning, (c) promoting collaboration among educators, and (d) improving educators' data-use skills.

RESEARCH RESULTS

Access to Data

Past research has indicated that many schools do not have a database that allows for easy access and analysis of data (Cizek, 2000; Holcomb, 1999; Wise et al., 1991). Their computer systems are outdated and inadequate, and appropriate user-friendly software for data analysis is not available (Bernhardt, 2004). According to Thorn (2001), data needs and uses across schools are very diverse, and school data are often in disparate forms and locations, making it difficult to organized into an efficient database for easy access and analysis. In a survey conducted by CRESST in 2003, 41% of the participants indicated that their schools or districts had not been able to get the data they needed (Chen, Heritage, Danish, Choi, & Lee, 2003).

QSP can increase schools' capacity to store and retrieve assessment data in various subject areas. During our interviews, 6 participants indicated that with QSP, their district or schools could store various student data in one place for easy retrieval and analysis, and teachers could access data on the Web and examine data themselves. For example, a school principal pointed out that before having access to QSP, his school had only an attendance database, which lacked the capacity to store student achievement data. Student achievement scores had been kept on paper, which inhibited data analysis. With access to QSP, for the first time, student achievement data were put into a computer to be stored electronically. Although the principal's focus at this point was only on statewide test scores, he had taken a first step in thinking about how QSP could help the school better attend to students' needs. He envisioned that QSP would enable him and his colleagues to compare student performance from different years to provide valuable information on how their students developed in different academic areas.

For other schools that already stored data electronically, QSP enabled them to put student data from different sources into one file for conducting descriptive or comparative analysis. A superintendent stated:

> I have done much more with data and data analysis the last year than I did probably the three previous years in the district just because of the ease of use. It's very easy-to-use software. It's step-by-step. Also the data [are] all in one place. In the past, it may have been all in my office, but maybe in four different file cabinets. To have to do that by hand as opposed to being able to do it electronically, it has saved me hours and hours, if not days, of time.

Similarly, a principal noted, "QSP would give us a broader spectrum in our database, really. We'd be able to do much more with it."

Some interviewees reported that QSP could enhance data accessibility for teachers, who could take ownership of the data and begin to use it to conduct investigations, generating their own questions and solving specific problems in their classrooms. A school principal noted, "I think what's exciting for me is having data and the manipulation of data readily available for teachers. We can start talking about data rather than anecdotes."

Another superintendent stated, "What we're trying to do with QSP is upgrade our capacity here for data compilation and data analysis. [The teachers] are using [data], but they would be using [data] at a higher level if they used QSP."

Identifying Students' Needs

With access to QSP, educators found they could collect and disaggregate data more efficiently to investigate the performance of different subgroups of students and to identify students who lagged behind in various subject areas. Based on the interview data from seven QSP users, we found that QSP helped educators examine both student achievement and background data, obtain test item-level information about a particular student's performance, focus on at-risk students by early identification and frequent monitoring, and take action to close the achievement gap.

At one school, the principal used QSP to generate a master list of all students in her school whose performance was below standard. After she identified the students who needed help, she was able to use QSP to pull out their individual math and reading scores on state tests. Once the groups of children with specific needs for each grade level were created, the principal presented the list and the QSP reports to the teachers. The student list, their test scores, and the QSP reports provided valuable information for the classroom teachers to focus on students' needs and to plan instruction tailored to individual students. The identified students were provided with additional instructional time with the teaching assistants. The principal commented:

> I was able to identify the children plus have their achievement level scores readily available in the list. With CTBS (Comprehensive Test of Basic Skills), all I would've been able to do is generate their scores, and then I would've had to go to our student information systems and pull out the children that fall under No Child Left Behind, and then come back and make a different list on my own. ... We have to know who they are, and we have to monitor them.

Using QSP to help schools identify students at risk appeared to be the top priority in a school's reform agenda. A principal noted:

> Basically we've been using it to determine—specifically looking at students who are not proficient, digging around and drilling down to find out what we can do as far as remediating them. That is basically where we've focused our attention.

At another school, at-risk students were identified using QSP and the school provides extra help to those students during after-school hours. A superintendent described QSP's applicability to after-school interventions:

> We have something that we call "Targeted Services." It's some things that we do after school for our students. [Building administrators] have utilized the QSP to basically generate some of the lists of those who are at risk of not being successful. That has helped them to extend to parents the invitation to, "Would you like to be involved in

this extra activity to help strengthen some of those skills that your children may not have?"

Educators indicated that another strength of QSP was its ability to provide test item-level information, which could help teachers pinpoint a specific area in a subject in which students were experiencing difficulties. One reading teacher pointed out that she was interested not only in general reading scores but also in each student group's performance on subcategories of reading, such as comprehension or vocabulary. With QSP, she could retrieve student information in a matter of seconds and disaggregate the data to find out which group of students needed more intervention in subcategories of reading skills. The information from QSP analysis guided her planning in reading curriculum and helped her tailor instruction to meet individual student's needs.

A superintendent stated that QSP allowed greater disaggregation of data:

to drill it down even one step further, not just the general assessment, but start to look at some of the subtests of that assessment to see if there are areas in their building or areas in our curriculum that we need to either change or reinforce or look for additional resources or provide some different remediation for our children.

A principal talked about how data analysis from QSP had increased differentiated instruction in the classroom:

What we've done is used it for directed instruction, more differentiation in the classroom ... using data analysis and more online real-time testing in order to be able to differentiate instruction for those various students so that we can focus on their particular strengths and weaknesses, particularly their weaknesses and try to remediate those, so that we can bring them up to proficiency.

To identify students' specific needs, some schools implementing QSP commented on the fact that, using QSP, they could examine both students' achievement data and their background data. Information such as student gender, cultural background, language proficiency, and attitude toward schooling can reveal students' habits and interests, which helps educators examine the multiple factors that contribute to student academic performance. From a superintendent, we learned that the teachers in his district were excited about using QSP to examine both student performance and background data simultaneously. As the superintendent pointed out, "Traditionally ... from the state, the data you get is the data you get, and there's no way you can look at it in any other way than the way they present it."

Research has shown the profound effect assessment has on focusing instruction and improving student learning (Black & Michel, 1998; Black & Wiliam, 1998a,

1998b; Glaser & Baxter, 1999; Herman, 2002; Shepard, 2000); students' learning in particular benefits when teachers use formative assessments (Black, Harrison, Lee, & Wiliam, 2001; Coffey, Sato, & Schneider, 2001). A promising practice in the area of formative assessment emerged during the process of QSP implementation. With easy storage of and access to different kinds of student data, some educators began to pay more attention to local, formative assessments, which could provide continual monitoring and interpretation of student performance. The decision makers at two schools became aware that annual testing does not provide the detailed information about students' learning needed by teachers to guide instruction, and that frequent local assessment can help teachers identify at-risk students early so they can benefit from academic intervention programs. One school implementing QSP reported "conducting biweekly assessment with at-risk students to gauge progress over time." With the assessment information, this school offered "a before-school math tutoring program" and "sent out to their parents home support activities" to involve parents in students' learning.

Another school was planning to import local assessment data into QSP so that they could examine student performance on both state- and classroom-level tests. A principal noted, "We also talked about how we could bring in other measures other than just our standardized test scores. One of the things that we wanted to be able to do was get some of our building-level assessments."

Even though this school district had not begun QSP implementation, the initial training workshop had opened new possibilities for teachers to examine multiple data sources to understand students' learning. In using QSP, teachers learned to pay attention to students' learning contexts and planned to collect other measures that could shed light on students' academic performance.

Among the districts or schools that were waiting for the data to be loaded into QSP system, five reported that after being introduced to QSP, they began to envision new ways of paying close attention to students' needs and designing new school improvement plans with student data. One school planned to "use QSP to accumulate student data over the years beginning from next year" so that eventually, the educators there could "conduct longitudinal analysis to examine student trends in learning." Another school was planning to use QSP to store and share student information across grades, so that "a fifth-grade teacher could have access to the test results from the fourth grade." Having information about each individual student before the beginning of the new semester enables teachers to plan instruction based on each individual student's performance in previous years.

One school principal described the school improvement plan to be implemented in the upcoming year once all the data have been imported into QSP:

> For example, we'll take in areas of economically disadvantaged students, we will identify their weaknesses, and then the Title I teachers and aides that work with those students will work to try to give them additional instruction in those weak areas.

In addition to allowing teachers to examine and manipulate data during summer, another school included administering periodic local assessments in its school improvement plan. Educators there set up goals to provide identification of and early intervention for at-risk students by examining both student performance data from previous years and data from local assessments in the next year.

Using QSP to Promote Collaboration

Past research has indicated that collaboration among educators is a key factor in promoting school change (Darling-Hammond, 1990; Marks & Louis, 1999; Spillane & Louis, 2002; Tighe, Wang, & Foley, 2002). The process of identifying and meeting students' needs requires a team effort; collaboration among professionals is essential for building school capacity to sustain the practices of using data for school improvement. In our study, it emerged that QSP acted as a catalyst for collaboration among school personnel. QSP afforded opportunities for inquiry and reflection among colleagues, which can have a great impact on improving achievement for all students (Hall & Hord, 2001). Interview data from nine users in our study showed that some districts and schools formed data-use teams in which participants worked together to make decisions about which data to collect or import, what questions to investigate, how to analyze data and present results, and what actions to take to improve instruction. At other schools, implementing QSP promoted cooperative work between technology support personnel and decision makers. Two schools were planning to use Web-based QSP to enhance communication between teachers and parents.

A school principal who participated in QSP training with two fourth-grade classroom teachers, the reading specialist, and the guidance counselor, described how, after the training, she and her colleagues worked collaboratively to discuss how they planned to implement QSP based on their school improvement plan:

> We came back to school, and we did talk about how we could use the program based on our school improvement plan, and ... the goals that we have for learning here, and how we would use that for instructional purposes.

A superintendent described how he had brought QSP reports to the monthly meetings with school principals to open up discussions for continuous school improvement:

> We meet in our Principal Meetings, [which] I call our "Instructional Leaders' Meetings." We meet monthly. Continuous improvement is one of the agenda items that are there every month, so we're always talking about the process. That's a logical place

to bring in some of the reports that I have generated, which I had done to share with the principals.

In addition to collaboration among educators, there was evidence of the importance of collaboration between IT personnel and decision makers. A district director of instruction emphasized that to get to the point of being able to use the data to plan for students' learning required the support of the technical department to clean the database, import the data, and provide QSP training to school principals and teachers.

Schools recognized that collaboration between parents and the school was important in meeting students' needs. Some schools were planning to utilize Web-based QSP to deliver more timely student progress reports to parents and to increase parental involvement in their students' learning. For example, one school is in the process of setting up accounts for parents so that they will have access to reports and to the digital portfolio. Another principal reported that:

> The Web-based component is very important to me. We have to do the progress reports. No matter when we put them out, there are always some parents who come back and say, "If we'd only known sooner, we could have helped and done something."

Training on Data Use

Effective data use that will lead to school improvement is dependent on the skills of education practitioners to collect and analyze data. Yet, the development of these skills has not routinely been a part of administrator preparation programs, and hardly ever a feature of teachers' pre-service and in-service training (Cromey, 2000; Herman & Gribbons, 2001).

Face-to-face or online training on QSP use and on conducting investigations based on student data had been provided to participants in the rollout. Two participants indicated that QSP training had changed their perception of what constitutes data and why data collection should be guided by research questions. One interviewee revealed that he had repeatedly advised colleagues in his school district not to input all kinds of data into the district database for analysis without giving serious consideration to the questions to be investigated. He observed that QSP training was effective in making people realize the role research questions play in the cycle of investigation; as a result, a more systematic approach to inputting data had been adopted. A QSP trainer informed us that providing face-to-face and online training on data use with QSP had sensitized school personnel to the value of data, changed their perception of what constituted data, and stimulated them to collect, store, and analyze data relevant to understanding student learning. In addition to learning the functionality of the QSP software, administrators and teachers developed practical skills in data collection, analysis, and interpretation, and gained confidence in conducting data-based inquiries to monitor student progress. A district director of technology noted:

> And I think finally at the training they saw the light that these were the only assessments they needed in the system and not try to put everything under the sun ... so that was, I think, a benefit of the training sessions. This will give them the understanding that it depends on the type of question and not just having all of the data and dumping it in.

CONCLUSION

Prior research has suggested that training educators to use existing data effectively and to collect local data can have a positive effect on student achievement and school improvement (Anderson & Postl, 2001; Khanna, Trousdale, Penuel, & Kell, 1999; Rubenstein & Wodatch, 2000; Ward, 1998). In the past, technical obstacles have stood in the way of effective data, especially difficulties in organizing data into an efficient database (Thorn, 2001). The results of the QSP study show that, with some basic training in data use and in a relatively brief period of implementation of a technology tool, educators became more aware of the value of data use for identifying students' needs. For some educators, this awareness began with the disaggregation of statewide test results by subgroups of students and by subscales as a means of identifying at-risk students. Others began from a recognition of the benefit of more frequent assessments to identify needs and monitor progress. Moreover, our study suggests that because educators had access to data and data analysis with QSP, they were more motivated to use information about their students and to provide interventions to meet the needs of at-risk students.

A key factor contributing to teachers' ability to focus instruction on what students need to learn next is assessment information (Black & Michel, 1998; Black & Wiliam, 1998a, 1998b; Glaser & Baxter, 1999; Herman 2002; Shepard, 2000). Indeed, projects focused on improving teachers' formative assessment practices have shown particular success (Black et al., 2001; Black, Harrison, Lee, Marshall, & Wiliam, 2003; Coffey et al., 2001). Although the QSP users were at the very early stages of using assessment information to plan for students' learning needs, the results from the study suggest that technology-supported data use has the potential to increase the capacity of practitioners to use summative and formative assessments to identify needs and focus instructional planning.

An increasing body of research suggests that the existence of a professional community that involves collaboration among its members is a key factor in promoting school change (Darling-Hammond, 1990; Joyce & Showers, 1995; Kruse & Louis, 1995; Louis & Marks, 1998; Marks & Louis, 1999; Newmann & Wehlage, 1995; Spillane & Louis, 2002; Tighe et al., 2002). The results of the QSP study highlight the importance of collaboration for data use in schools and districts, not only among educators, but also between educators and technical personnel, underscoring the fact that the process of identifying and meeting students' needs requires a team effort and cannot be undertaken by one person alone. Moreover, because of the turnover in personnel, expertise in technology-supported data use cannot reside with a few people. Our research also indicates that collaboration is essential for building capacity to embed and sustain the practices of using data in schools and districts.

In a number of cases, collaboration expanded beyond the professional community to include parents. Educators wanted to use QSP to more closely involve parents in their children's learning by sending frequent progress reports home and permitting parents to access vital student data using a Web-based interface.

A strong research base on technology-supported data use in schools and districts, specifically with reference to identifying at-risk students, does not yet exist. The study of QSP implementation points to some of the potential benefits of using technology to identify and monitor students' needs. Further research will be needed on data use supported by technology in a number of areas. First, it will be important for researchers to investigate the extent to which educators sustain data-use practices that are supported by technology, as well as the degree to which they increase their skills in data analysis. Second, longitudinal studies are needed to examine the effects of these practices on student achievement, particularly on the achievement of at-risk students. Third, investigations of teacher data use supported by technology are needed to understand the impact of teachers having easy access to a wide range of data, both summative and formative, on their instructional practices. Fourth, research is needed to examine if access to and analysis of electronic data by school personnel supports the development of professional communities in schools and promotes networks of shared purpose that expand and deepen the dialogue about student learning.

REFERENCES

American Educational Research Association. (2000, July). *High-stakes testing in preK–12 education.* Retrieved April 25, 2005, from http://www.aera.net/policyandprograms/?id=378

American Educational Research Association, American Psychological Association, and National Council on Measurement in Education. (1999). *Standards for educational and psychological testing.* Washington, DC: American Educational Research Association.

Anderson, B., & Postl, B. (2001, April). *Using large data sets as a basis for school improvement.* Paper presented at the annual meeting of the American Educational Research Association, Seattle, WA.

Baker, E. L. (2001). Testing and assessment: A progress report. *Educational Assessment, 7*(1), 1–12.

Baker, E. L. (2003). *From usable to useful assessment knowledge: A design problem* (CSE Tech. Rep. No. 612). Los Angeles: University of California, National Center for Research on Evaluation, Standards, and Student Testing.

Baker, E. L., Linn, R. L., Herman, J. L., & Koretz, D. (2002, Winter). *Standards for educational accountability systems* (CRESST Policy Brief No. 5). Los Angeles: University of California, National Center for Research on Evaluation, Standards, and Student Testing.

Bernhardt, V. (2004). *Data analysis for continuous school improvement.* Larchmont, NY: Eye on Education.

Berrueta-Clement, J. R., Schweinhart, L. J., Barnett, W. S., Epstein, A. S., & Weikart, D. P. (1984). *Changed lives: The effects of the Perry Preschool Program on youths through age 19.* Ypsilanti, MI: The High/Scope Press.

Black, P., Harrison, C., Lee, C., & Wiliam, D. (2001, April). *Theory and practice in the development of formative assessment.* Paper presented at the annual meeting of the American Educational Research Association, Seattle, WA.

Black, P., Harrison, C., Lee, C., Marshall, B., & Wiliam, D. (2003). *Assessment for learning: Putting it into practice.* New York: Open University Press.

Black, P., & Michel, A. (Eds.). (1996). *Learning from pupil assessment: International comparisons.* Monographs of the Center for the Study of Evaluation, University of California, *12*.

Black, P., & Wiliam, D. (1998a). Assessment and classroom learning. *Assessment in Education, 5*(1), 7–74.

Black, P., & Wiliam, D. (1998b). Inside the black box: Raising standards through classroom assessment. *Phi Delta Kappan, 80,* 139–148.

Black, P., & Wiliam, D. (2004). The formative purpose: Assessment must first promote learning. In M. Wilson (Ed.), *Towards coherence between classroom assessment and accountability* (p. 22). Chicago: University of Chicago Press.

Bryant, D. M., & Maxwell, K. (1997). The effectiveness of early intervention for disadvantaged children. In M. J. Guralnick (Ed.), *The effectiveness of early intervention* (pp. 23–46). Baltimore: Brookes.

Campbell, F. A., & Ramey, C. T. (1995). Cognitive and school outcomes for high-risk African American students in middle adolescence: Positive effects of early intervention. *American Educational Research Journal, 32,* 743–772.

Choppin, J. (2002, April). *Data use in practice: Examples from the school level.* Paper presented at the annual meeting of the American Educational Research Association, New Orleans, LA. Retrieved April 22, 2002, from http://www.wcer.wisc.edu/mps/AERA2002/data_use_in_practice.htm

Cizek, G. J. (2000). Pockets of resistance in the assessment revolution. *Educational Measurement: Issues and Practices, 19*(2), 16–33.

Coffey, C., Sato, M., & Schneider, B. (2001, April). *Classroom assessment up close—and personal.* Paper presented at the annual meeting of the American Educational Research Association, Seattle, WA.

Cromey, A. (2000). Using student assessment data: What can we learn from schools? *Policy Issues, 6.* (ERIC Document Reproduction Service No. ED452593)

Darling-Hammond, L. (1990). Teacher professionalism: Why and how. In A. Lieberman (Ed.), *Schools as collaborative cultures: Creating the future now* (pp. 25–50). Bristol, PA: Falmer.

Dewey, J. (1897). My pedagogic creed. *The School Journal, 54*(3), 77–80. Retrieved December 7, 2004, from http://www.infed.org/archives/e-texts/e-dew-pc.htm

Garber, H. L. (1988). *The Milwaukee Project: Prevention of mental retardation in children at risk.* Washington, DC: American Association on Mental Retardation.

Glaser, R., & Baxter, G. P. (1999, September). *Assessing active knowledge.* Paper presented at the annual meeting of the National Center for Research on Evaluation, Standards, and Student Testing, University of California, Los Angeles.

Hall, G. E., & Hord, S. M. (2001). *Implementing change: Patterns, principles, and potholes.* Boston: Allyn & Bacon.

Herman, J., & Gribbons, B., (2001). *Lessons learned in using data to support school inquiry and continuous improvement: Final report to the Stuart Foundation* (CSE Tech. Rep. No. 535). Los Angeles: University of California, National Center for Research on Evaluation, Standards, and Student Testing.

Herman, J. L. (2002). *Instructional effects in elementary schools* (CSE Tech. Rep. No. 577). Los Angeles: University of California, National Center for Research on Evaluation, Standards, and Student Testing.

Holcomb, E. L. (1999). *Getting excited about data: How to combine people, passion, and proof.* Thousand Oaks, CA: Corwin.

Jester, R. E., & Guinagh, B. J. (1983). The Gordon Parent Education Infant and Toddler Program. In Consortium for Longitudinal Studies (Ed.), *As the twig is bent ... Lasting effects of preschool programs* (pp. 103–132). Hillsdale, NJ: Lawrence Erlbaum Associates, Inc.

Johnson, D. L., & Walker, T. (1991). A follow-up evaluation of the Houston Parent-Child Development Center: School performance. *Journal of Early Intervention, 15,* 226–236.

Joyce, B., & Showers, B. (1995). *Student achievement through staff development: Fundamentals of school renewal* (2nd ed.). White Plains, NY: Longman.

Khanna, R., Trousdale, D., Penuel, W. R., & Kell, J. (1999, April). *Supporting data use among administrators: Results from a data planning model.* Paper presented at the annual meeting of the American Educational Research Association, Montreal, Quebec, Canada.

Kruse, S., & Louis, K. S. (1995). Developing professional community in new and restructuring schools. In K. S. Louis, S. Kruse & Associates (Eds.), *Professionalism and community: Perspectives on reforming urban schools* (pp. 187–207). Thousand Oaks, CA: Corwin Press

Lally, J. R., Mangione, P. L., & Honig, A. S. (1988). The Syracuse University Family Development Research Program: Long-range impact on an early intervention with low-income children and their families. In I. E. Sigel (Series Ed.) & D. R. Powell (Vol. Ed.), *Annual advances in applied developmental psychology: Vol. 3. Parent education as early childhood intervention: Emerging directions in theory, research, and practice* (pp. 79–104). Norwood, NJ: Ablex.

Louis, K. S., Kruse, S., & Associates. (1995). *Professionalism and community: Perspectives on reforming urban schools.* Thousand Oaks, CA: Corwin.

Louis, K. S., & Marks, H. (1998). Does professional community affect the classroom? Teachers' work and student work in restructuring schools. *American Journal of Education, 106,* 532–575.

Lyon, G. R. (2002, June). *Learning disabilities & early intervention strategies: How to reform the special education referral & identification process.* Statement before the House Committee on Education and the Workforce Subcommittee on Education Reform. Retrieved December 2, 2003, from U.S. Department of Health & Human Services Web site: http://www.hhs.gov/asl/testify/t020606a.html

Marks, H., & Louis, K. S. (1999). Teacher empowerment and the capacity for organizational learning. *Education Administration Quarterly, 35,* 751–781.

National Research Council. [Pellegrino, J. W., Chudowsky, N., Glaser, R., (Eds.)]. (2001). *Knowing what students know: The science and design of educational assessment.* Washington, DC: National Academy Press.

Newmann, F. M., & Wehlage, G. G. (1995). *Successful school restructuring: A report to the public and educators.* Madison: University of Wisconsin, Wisconsin Center for Education Research, Center on Organization and Restructuring of Schools.

Rubenstein, M. C., & Wodatch, J. K. (2000). *Stepping up to the challenge: Case studies of educational improvement in Title I secondary schools.* Washington, DC: U.S. Department of Education, Office of the Undersecretary, Planning, and Evaluation Service, Elementary and Secondary Education Division.

Shepard, L. (2000). *The role of classroom assessment in teaching and learning* (CSE Tech. Rep. No. 517). Los Angeles: University of California, National Center for Research on Evaluation, Standards, and Student Testing.

Shepard, L. A. (2004). Curricular coherence in assessment design. In M. Wilson (Ed.), *Towards coherence between classroom assessment and accountability: Part II* (pp. 239–249). Chicago: University of Chicago Press.

Smithson, J. L., & Porter, A. C. (2004). From policy to practice: The evolution of one approach to describing and using curriculum data. In M. Wilson (Ed.), *Towards coherence between classroom assessment and accountability: Part II* (pp. 105–131). Chicago: University of Chicago Press.

Spillane, J. P., & Louis, K. S. (2002). School improvement processes and practices: Professional learning for building instructional capacity. In J. Murphy (Ed.), *The educational leadership challenge: Redefining leadership for the 21st century* (pp. 83–104). Chicago: University of Chicago Press.

Stiggins, R. J. (2002). Assessment crisis: The absence of assessment for learning. *Phi Delta Kappan, 83*, 758–765. Retrieved August 25, 2004, from http://www.pdkintl.org/kappan/k0206sti.htm

Thorn, C. A. (2001). Knowledge management for educational information systems: What is the state of the field? *Education Policy Analysis Archives, 9*(47). Retrieved August 25, 2004, from http://epaa.asu.edu/epaa/v9n47/

Tighe, E., Wang, A., & Foley, E. (2002). *An analysis of the effect of Children Achieving on student achievement in Philadelphia elementary schools*. Philadelphia: Consortium for Policy Research in Education.

U.S. Department of Education. (2001). *Twenty-third annual report to Congress on the implementation of the Individuals with Disabilities Education Act*. Washington, DC: Author.

Ward, M. (1998, April). *A systems approach to middle school evaluation: Guilford County Schools' formative approach*. Paper presented at the annual meeting of the American Educational Research Association, San Diego, CA.

Wayman, J. C., Stringfield, S., & Yakimowski, M. (2004). Software enabling school improvement through analysis of student data (Rep. No. 67). Baltimore: Johns Hopkins University, Center for Research on the Education of Students Placed At Risk.

Wise, S. L., Lukin, L. E., & Roos, L. L. (1991). Teacher beliefs about training in testing and measurement. *Journal of Teacher Education, 42*(1), 37–42.

Practices That Support Data Use in Urban High Schools

Mary Ann Lachat and Stephen Smith
Center for Resource Management, Inc.

This article presents initial findings of a case study focusing on data use in five low-performing urban high schools undergoing comprehensive schoolwide reform. The case study investigates: (a) the ways in which disaggregated data can be used to examine progress and guide improvement in the process of restructuring urban, low-performing high schools; (b) factors and conditions that either promote or act as barriers to data use; and (c) the policy and practice implications of achieving effective data use in a high school reform process. Study findings point to several key factors that have an impact on data use in the study sites: the quality and accuracy of available data, staff access to timely data, the capacity for data disaggregation, the collaborative use of data organized around a clear set of questions, and leadership structures that support schoolwide use of data. The findings build on current literature and also contribute new knowledge of the key roles played by a data team and a data coach in fostering effective data use in high school reform.

The high school reform movement is drawing increasing attention to the need for more systematic uses of data to inform the policy, management, and instructional changes that result in higher student achievement. As today's educators grapple with the challenge of changing current high school structures into more effective learning environments, data can be a powerful ally in stimulating positive change and improvement. In low-performing urban high schools, increasing demands for accountability are paralleled by equity concerns arising from the enormous diversity of the student population—in culture, language, prior educational experiences, home situations, learning styles, attitudes toward learning, and future aspirations.

Requests for reprints should be sent to Mary Ann Lachat, Center for Resource Management, Inc., 200 International Drive, Suite 201, Portsmouth, NH 03801. E-mail: MALachat@crminc.com

The twin mandates of equity and accountability have made it imperative that educators base decisions on accurate and meaningful data about student learning and achievement (Johnson, 2002; Lachat, 2002). To create high schools that are responsive to diversity, connected to the realities of today's world, and driven by a focus on success for all students, more systemic reform strategies are needed, and new capacities must be developed. One of these capacities is the strategic use of data to support student success and school improvement (Bernhardt, 2000a; Codding & Rothman, 1999).

The Northeast and Islands Regional Educational Laboratory (LAB) at Brown University is conducting a case study that investigates the process and effects of high school restructuring in five low-performing urban high schools that are implementing three central elements of systemic reform: (a) establishing smaller and more personalized learning environments, (b) shifting to standards-based curriculum and instruction, and (c) using data to support continuous improvement. The case study component focusing on data use in the high school reform process is being conducted by the Center for Resource Management, Inc. (CRM), a partner organization of the LAB. This article summarizes some initial findings of this study component. The purpose of the article is to present illustrative case study evidence that contributes to deeper understandings of conditions and practices that either promote or act as barriers to the use of data as a central element of school reform in urban, low-performing high schools.

DATA-DRIVEN SCHOOL REFORM

Our examination of data use in five low-performing high schools builds on an emerging body of research and school reform literature that cites the importance of data-driven decision making in creating more effective schools (Armstrong & Anthes, 2001; Bernhardt, 1998, 2000a; Killion & Bellamy, 2000; Schwartz, 2002). Effective use of data by district and school personnel is increasingly identified as a central tenet in school improvement processes (Chrispeels, 1992; Earl & Katz, 2002; Protheroe, 2001; Wayman & Stringfield, 2003), not only to raise test scores (Kennedy, 2003), but also to change school cultures and teacher attitudes (Feldman & Tung, 2001), especially toward low-performing, at-risk students (Armstrong & Anthes, 2001). Johnson (1996, 2002) examined many uses of data as a major force in building school and district capacity to educate students equitably and reduce achievement gaps. The research and practice literature has shown, however, that several key factors influence data use: the types of data available to school staff; technology and data-system capacity; and school conditions and practices that either promote or act as barriers to staff use of data.

Data available to schools. Schools and districts generally collect a wide array of data in three primary categories related to student demographics, school and educational program data, and performance data. Although the range of data available to schools is extensive, it is rarely used effectively (Wayman & Stringfield, 2003). Schools that want to use data to drive their decisions often don't know where to begin or what type of data to use (American Association of School Administrators [AASA], 2002). There is often too much data, but not the right type or not in a format that facilitates use (Schmoker, 2003). Data often aren't available to school staff when they need it, and the often complex and confusing formats of data reports make it more difficult for them to sort through what is most useful for them (Lachat, 2002; National Education Association Foundation for the Improvement of Education [NFIE], 2003). In attempting to use data, schools often employ the wrong type of data, using indirect measures of learning for which they have no explanatory model to interpret the data (Marzano, 2003). Teachers often use data meant for compliance when what they need is timely, diagnostic data on the students they teach (Olson, 2002; Rudner & Boston, 2003).

Descriptive cases of how schools use data for school improvement (Mason, 2002) have noted that the types of data collected determine the types of decisions that are made. In Mason's (2002) study of the use of data for school improvement, six schools instituted data-driven strategies to improve students' state assessment scores. The data that were most useful to these schools were a combination of assessment, demographic, perception, and education program data. Pardini (2000) noted that teachers are better able to modify their instructional strategies when they have current information about the skill levels and proficiencies of their students. Researchers also suggest the importance of teacher use of varied types of data, including video analysis, classroom observations, and student work samples (NFIE, 2003; North Central Regional Educational Laboratory [NCREL], 2003). Prior studies also have suggested that multiple methods of data collection should be used (Brimijoin, Marquissee, & Tomlinson, 2003).

Technology and data system capacity. Researchers and leaders of school reform efforts have cited the capacity for data disaggregation as being essential to effective data use (Bernhardt, 2000b; Holcomb, 1999; Johnson, 2002; Love, 2000). High-level data disaggregation requires the capability to integrate or link multiple types of student performance data, demographic data, and data on students' educational experiences. However, even in districts where extensive data are maintained, the technology to integrate and manipulate different types of data is lacking (Wayman, Stringfield, & Yakimowski, 2004). Visher and Hudis (1999) reported that very few high schools participating in the New American High Schools initiative had the information system capacity to link student results to specific programs, classroom practices, and learning environments.

Data generally exist in multiple electronic files that include the district data system as well as data files from state assessments and other testing programs. This means that teachers and administrators may not have easy access to the data they need to examine how students enrolled in particular programs are performing on various measures, nor are they able to determine the effects of programs and practices on student performance over time (Lachat & Williams, 2003).

In their analysis of currently available technology, Wayman et al. (2004) noted that recent technological advances in data-warehousing applications have produced software tools that integrate multiple student data files. They recommended that schools move toward data-warehousing capability to support the analysis and use of data. Other researchers have also cited the increasing importance of more advanced data-system technology, as well as the need to present data in formats that are meaningful to school leaders and teachers (Rudner & Boston, 2003; Schwartz, 2002; Streifer, 2002; Thorn, 2001). Although technology may be available, however, school districts often lack the funds or do not allocate the resources necessary to establish coherent and high-level data-system capability (Olson, 2002). Mason (2002) also emphasized that technology capacity alone is not the answer; such capacity needs to be coupled with teacher willingness and capacity to use data. Teachers need to learn how to obtain and manage data, ask good questions, accurately analyze data, and apply data results appropriately and ethically.

Supporting data use. A study by Armstrong and Anthes (2001) highlighted several elements associated with effective data use: strong leadership, a districtwide culture that supports the use of data for continuous improvement, a structure for supporting and training teachers to use data, a close accounting of every student's performance on academic standards, and a well-defined, data-driven school improvement process. A process that involves teachers in data analysis is essential, and Wade (2001) emphasized that as many teachers as possible are needed to support effective data use in schools. Data use is most effective when teacher decisions about instructional effectiveness are based on assessments of students' actual proficiencies in various skill areas (Pardini, 2000). A data-driven inquiry process can act as a tool for change in schools often considered furthest from current standards of excellence (Holcomb, 1999, 2001).

Data-use strategies that involve school staff in collaborative problem solving can foster the open dialogue needed for equity issues to be addressed (Love, 2000). Inquiry-based schools promote a culture of high standards and the use of appropriate assessments for improving student learning (Rallis & MacMullen, 2000). Some researchers have highlighted the use of questions to structure teacher analysis of data as a key element to effective data use (NCREL, 2003; Protheroe, 2001). Ideally, teachers should be provided with opportunities to work collaboratively in building their capacity to use data (NFIE, 2003). A study of 18 Annenberg Challenge Schools in six states noted successes in the use of data-driven strategies where teachers worked collaboratively in framing questions to monitor school progress in implementing new practices (Keeney, 1998). Another study highlighted the need to provide time for teachers to meet and review assessment data in making instructional decisions (Cromey, 2000).

Barriers to data use. Many reasons for the lack of data use in schools center on the lack of training, cultural resistance, and fear of reprisal. Few administrators and teachers have had formal training or experience in analyzing and interpreting data or using assessment results for program and instructional improvement (Bernhardt, 2000b; Cizek, 2000). There is minimal preservice emphasis on the use of data in school reform (Cromey, 2000), and most schools do not provide teachers with the ongoing, sustained training they need to ask the right questions in analyzing and interpreting data (Protheroe, 2001).

In her extensive examination of data use in schools, Love (2000) showed that schools are ill-equipped to use data to address problems, target improvements, or monitor progress. They lack the staff skills, time, and organizational structures to use data effectively. Bernhardt (2000b) noted that most schools conduct their education programs with little analysis of how well programs work for students, and rely instead on "gut feelings" about what is and isn't working. Cultural resistance is a significant barrier to data use in high schools. High school cultures simply do not focus on data analysis, and the use of data for ongoing decision making and program improvement represents a major cultural shift (Lachat, 2002; Visher & Hudis, 1999).

Changing a school's culture and building teacher capacity to use data often require a change in staff attitudes toward the diverse student populations in a school, as well as the skills to apply appropriate interventions for students based on data. In a study examining teacher attitudes toward the potential success of previously low-performing students, Armstrong and Anthes (2001) noted that teachers find it difficult to link data to an appropriate intervention. In their study, the researchers determined that teacher use of data helped clear up false assumptions. However, even when teachers are given training and time to think about using data to inform their practices, they may be reluctant to do so in a culture where they feel threatened or fear they will be attacked for something they are doing or not doing in the classroom (Bernhardt, 2000b). Effective data use requires a culture that is driven by inquiry, not fear.

METHODOLOGY FOR THE STUDY

This case study of data use in high school reform reflects the growing emphasis on the use of disaggregated data to monitor school progress in raising student achievement. This emphasis has been driven by both federal and state accountability mandates. The purpose of the case study is to investigate: (a) the ways in which disaggregated data can be used to examine progress and guide improvement in the process of restructuring urban, low-performing high schools; (b) factors and conditions that either promote or act as barriers to data use; and (c) the policy and practice implications of achieving effective data use in a high school reform process. Research in this area is limited, and few studies have produced case study evidence of the multiple factors associated with the use of disaggregated data to improve student learning and achievement in urban, low-performing high schools. The study is thus intended to build on the current literature and to provide evidence of data use in high school reform that can serve as a foundation for future research.

Study Sites

The case study is being conducted in five low-performing high schools located in three high-poverty urban districts. The size of the student population across the five schools ranged from approximately 1,400 students to 1,800 students. In four of the high schools, Hispanic students represented slightly more than half of the student population. Three of the high schools were part of a district-driven high school reform process. However, although located in the same district, the schools exhibited very different cultures, and they varied considerably in their leadership structures. These schools offered the opportunity to examine variations in data use in high schools operating under the same strong district mandates for high school reform. A fourth high school site was one of five high schools in a district where there was an overall district plan for reform, but reform decisions were largely site-based. The fifth high school site was the only public high school in its district.

Site selection criteria were aligned with the LAB's mission of advancing research knowledge of effective reform strategies in high-poverty, low-performing high schools and conducting research in school settings where reform plans reflect a clear commitment to the concurrent implementation of three core reform components. These components are establishing smaller learning communities (SLCs); implementing standards-based curriculum and instruction; and using data to support continuous improvement. The schools chosen for the case study met these criteria. As such, they were not randomly selected.

Although this is a limitation of the study, all of the schools share the trait of being large, comprehensive high schools in urban, high-poverty areas. Each contains a diverse student population with many students not performing at grade level on state-mandated assessments. Although the schools are not a statistically representative sample, they can be considered typical of many low-performing medium to large urban high schools. The limited sample of only five high schools in the Northeast makes generalizability to other high schools more difficult, but certainly not invalid, as the literature suggests that many high schools across the nation struggle with the same issues as these five schools.

Study Procedures

Over a 4-year period, an extensive array of qualitative data was collected to examine the process of data use in the five study sites and to provide contextual evidence of factors that either supported or inhibited the use of data. Qualitative data sources include: (a) school reform documents, such as Education Improvement Plans, showing uses of data for planning and improvement; (b) field note documentation of the numerous data analysis meetings that occurred in the schools, including a running record of decisions and actions that resulted from data use; (c) an archival catalogue of data used by the schools; and (d) interviews with principals and other school administrators, teachers, and school design teams and data teams.

Qualitative data were entered into NVivo, a qualitative data-management program selected because of its flexibility and power to support the coding and manipulation of the qualitative data. The findings reported in this article are based on initial analyses of the extensive field note data collected over the 4 years of the study, the archival catalogue of data used by school staff, and group interviews with school design teams and data teams. The full report summarizing all of the case study evidence will be completed by the fall of 2005.

Qualitative procedures included the use of a data coach as an external facilitator across the study sites who also functioned as a participant observer member of the research team. In addition to providing technical assistance, the data coach was able to maintain an ongoing presence in the schools over the 4-year period and collected detailed field note documentation of data use in the schools. The rationale for the use of a data coach as part of the study design was based on emerging research showing the importance of external facilitators or coaches in school change processes (Center for Collaborative Education, 2002, 2003; RAND Corporation, 2002). There is growing support for the role of coaches in multiple aspects of school reform (Greene, 2004). However, although the literature cites the use of coaches to support schoolwide change, instructional improvement, and literacy, there is limited case evidence of the role of a coach in supporting data use. Our case study thus contributes to this new area of knowledge. It is also important to note that because of each high school's emphasis on data use as an integral aspect of their reform process, all of them had established a school team with assigned responsibility for data analysis and data dissemination. They tended to be called *data teams*, which is also the term used to describe them in this article.

The full study also will report on changes that occurred on multiple indicators of student performance in the study sites. A longitudinal (4-year) research database has been created to support this analysis. The application used to create the longitudinal student database was CRM's Socrates Data System, a data-warehousing application that integrates data from school administrative systems, state assessment data files, standardized test files, and other data sources. The system creates a fully integrated database that links all relevant information about the student and allows extensive data disaggregation. It was specifically designed to support data integration, data management, and research/program evaluation functions. Socrates was used in the study because it not only supported research functions, but also provided a technology tool for establishing data-system capacity at each site that was essential to a study of data use by school personnel.

As noted in the research findings described earlier in this article, in spite of federal mandates that call for fuller use of disaggregated data, many districts and schools lack the technology to disaggregate student performance data (Lachat & Williams, 2003; Rudner & Boston, 2003; Schwartz, 2002; Streifer, 2002; Thorn, 2001; Wayman et al., 2004). This was true for the study sites as well. Therefore, the rationale for providing data-system technical assistance was to create equal capacity across the five high school sites in establishing school access to disaggregated data that was essential to the focus of this study. The case study could then focus on how each of the schools actually used data for decision making, as well as the factors that affected data use. Socrates was used to create a fully integrated relational database for each of the study sites that brought together data from the district information system and data from state assessments and other testing programs. The database linked multiple types of student performance data to demographic data, student program data, and membership in an SLC. This allowed data to be disaggregated by these variables.

STUDY FINDINGS

The case study findings presented in this article are drawn from initial analyses conducted to examine the factors and conditions that either supported or acted as barriers to data use in the high school sites. The evidence discussed relates to four key factors that had an impact on data use: (a) data quality and data access, (b) capacity for data disaggregation, (c) collaborative use of data organized around a clear set of questions, and (d) leadership structures that enhanced data use.

Data Quality and Data Access

Integrating data use into the high school reform process meant that school teams needed timely access to accurate data from district information systems that were maintained centrally, with data entered at the school level. This was a challenge for all of the study sites. The districts and schools didn't recognize the extent to which data in their student information systems were not complete and/or accurate until they had to use data more rigorously. The most common data quality issues uncovered by more frequent use of the data files were tied to the high level of student mobility and high dropout rates between the 9th and 10th grades in these urban districts. In many cases, procedures at the school and district levels for updating data systems, accurately coding students who had left the system, and removing them from the "currently enrolled" student population files were not in place or not followed consistently by personnel. In all of the sites, it took the combined efforts of both district and school personnel to resolve these issues, which in turn had the effect of improving teacher and administrator perceptions of the accuracy and relevance of data provided to them.

The case study also revealed the combination of factors that need to be addressed to resolve the issue of schools having timely access to pertinent data in urban settings. This issue reflects previous literature that cites the lack of information at the right time and in the right formats as a major barrier to data use in schools (NFIE, 2003; Schmoker, 2003). In all of the study sites, district data-system personnel were burdened with data requests from multiple projects, often without being informed of how the data would be used. Developing better understandings with them about the data the schools needed and when the data were needed became an important strategy for improving school access to data. The issue was most effectively resolved for the three high schools located in the same district, where a formal Data Access Plan was developed in collaboration with district data-system personnel. By the 3rd year of the study, these schools were getting a much faster turn-around on quarterly attendance and course grade data disaggregated down to the level of the SLC and 9th-grade team structures that had been created in the schools. School teams also were receiving disaggregated state assessment and other standardized test data as early as possible. This allowed them to use the data more effectively to determine the school's progress in improving literacy skills and to target instruction more effectively for the students assigned to a particular learning community.

The establishment of a 9th-grade interdisciplinary team structure was a major strategy used by all of the high schools to create smaller and more personalized learning environments for students. Because of the pressure on these teams to demonstrate positive results for students, the teachers wanted information on the characteristics and past performance of the incoming 9th-grade students assigned to their learning community as close to the opening of school as possible. The process of creating timely access to these data illustrates the fundamental connection between data-system capacity and data use. In all but one of the high schools, the 9th-grade population came from several district middle schools, and data were not readily available at the opening of school on the characteristics of the students, absence levels for the previous year, previous test performance in reading and mathematics, and 8th-grade state assessment results.

Significant changes had to be made in each school district's schedule for assigning students to SLCs, processing pertinent Grade 8 data, and making data on the incoming freshmen available to high schools. The lack of sufficient district data personnel slowed the process down for two of the high schools. Still, by the 4th year of the study, all of the high school 9th-grade teams were getting data on a far more timely basis than in the past. Data were used to address equity in SLC membership, student attendance issues, and literacy. Administrators were able to determine whether SLCs within a school were similar to each other in the demographic characteristics of their students, an important equity goal. Teacher teams reviewed absence data on the incoming freshmen to determine whether school attendance was an immediate issue they would have to address for their students. In two of the high schools, the 9th-grade teacher teams used disaggregated state assessment results to specifically identify students who had achieved or were close to achieving standards in reading skills, as well as those students who clearly needed intensive interventions.

Data Disaggregation

The study findings affirm current research that cites the capacity for data disaggregation as being essential to effective data use (Bernhardt, 2000a; Holcomb, 1999; Johnson, 2002; Love, 2000). All of the high schools had previously received student-performance data with minimal or no disaggregation. The fully integrated database that was created for each site provided the capacity to disaggregate data by combinations of demographic characteristics, SLC assignment, participation in specific programs, and exposure to specific literacy or other instructional interventions. This allowed more targeted uses of data to address student performance issues in these low-performing high schools.

SLC staff received quarterly data showing the extent to which they were having an impact on reducing poor attendance and course failure rates. The use of disaggregated data also helped overcome a narrow over-reliance on aggregated state assessment and standardized test results. When the results of these measures were disaggregated in different ways, they became more meaningful to school staff and were used more meaningfully in making instructional decisions.

School teams also came to realize that disaggregated data were "their" data; this data could be used to answer their questions. In one high school, student performance on state assessments and other standardized measures were disaggregated by frequency of student absence to allow school staff to examine their assumption that low achievement on these measures resulted from high student absence rates. The data showed not only that the students with low attendance rates were performing at failing levels, but also that the same was true for the majority of students with high attendance. The data thus confirmed that the school had two problems—student attendance and quality of instruction. Reviewing the data and eliminating teacher assumptions that the problem was only an attendance issue allowed for more productive discussions about the content and quality of instruction provided to students, teacher expectations, and the ways in which the SLCs might engage students more effectively in instruction as well as school attendance.

Consistency in grading across subject areas within SLC teams and within subject areas across SLC teams was another issue that was examined through the use of disaggregated data. Conversations among school teams and subject-area departments about grading criteria led to the question of how students' course grades related to their performance on state assessments and standardized tests. Data were disaggregated to show these relationships for the content areas of English/language arts and mathematics. What school staff discovered was that many students who had been given high grades were performing at the lower levels of the state assessments and other standardized tests. School teams started to recognize that these questions were connected to the more complex issues they faced in their school reform efforts—whether course offerings and grading criteria were aligned with standards, and whether instruction was sufficiently focused on the higher level proficiencies that were being measured in the state assessments. In three of the high schools, this led to school staff identifying the need for professional development related to such areas as rubric-based grading criteria and high-quality student work products. In another high school, a decision was made to start the development of common examinations across subject area course sections to ensure more consistency in teacher expectations for student performance.

Collaborative Inquiry

The case study confirmed that the practice of collaborative data use organized around a clear set of questions is a potent strategy for building staff skills and keeping the focus on student learning and achievement. This approach is supported in the literature (Holcomb, 1999, 2001; Love, 2000; NCREL, 2003; Protheroe, 2001; Rallis & MacMullen, 2000). However, evidence from three of the high schools also suggests that the process of organizing data use around clearly focused questions is far more powerful if it is established and championed as a schoolwide practice by school leaders—the principal and other administrators, teacher leaders, department chairs, and school coaches. Their modeling of the use of questions to focus the collaborative examination of data is a key factor in reinforcing this approach to schoolwide data use. Focusing on a set of key student performance questions not only builds staff skills to analyze data, but also increases their motivation to use the data.

When the high school teams collaboratively developed clearly focused questions, it helped them look beyond the data to examine other pertinent information, and they were far more likely to understand what the data meant for school improvement. The questioning process allowed staff who represented different perspectives in a school—administrator, teacher, guidance counselor, coach—to step back and consider more objectively how school policies, teacher beliefs, conditions for learning, or teaching practices might be affecting students' learning and achievement. When the data revealed false assumptions or hunches about specific groups of students, it became easier to get school staff to recognize the importance of basing decisions on objective data. The use of questions helped school teams maintain a focus on student achievement and ways in which the high school program needed to improve.

Leadership Structures That Support Data Use

The case study provided evidence of the mutual roles school leaders can play in fostering widespread use of data in high schools. In the two high schools in which data use was most effective, the use of data was strongly influenced by the leadership of the principal. It was also influenced by the shared leadership roles played by other administrators and teacher leaders in the schools. The involvement of assistant principals, SLC directors, department chairs, and teacher leaders from the interdisciplinary 9th-grade teams also was essential in establishing multiple types of data use in the schools. Transition coaches and instructional/literacy coaches provided follow-up assistance to various data users in the school and also played an important role in motivating teachers to use data. In addition, the combined strategy of using a data team and a data coach underscored the importance of the facilitator role in sustaining a focus on data use in the midst of extensive high school restructuring. Not all principals, even if they support data use, have all of the skills or time needed to move the process forward productively, especially in high school settings where the restructuring process is particularly complex and demanding.

Although two of the high schools had particularly high-functioning data teams, the case examples across all of the study sites contributed new knowledge about the role this type of school team can play in high school reform. The activities of the data teams were central to increasing communication among school staff about the trends and issues shown in the data. Because data team members were peers of other school staff, they played a key role in overcoming staff perceptions that data were inaccurate or not relevant to teacher concerns. Key tasks of the data teams included helping to improve the quality and accuracy of school-level data files, ensuring the timely retrieval of data from the district, disseminating data to different groups in the school, helping staff analyze and interpret data, targeting and monitoring goals for improvement, and responding to additional data requests by school staff.

The case study provided evidence about the collaborative role of a data coach in guiding a high school's transition toward a culture where data are used strategically throughout the school. It also contributed new knowledge about this aspect of coaching in high school reform. The data coach was a coach in the true sense in that various uses of data were modeled, but school staff were responsible for the analysis and interpretation of the data. Documentation of how the schools used the coaching assistance shed light on the importance of the coaching role in helping school staff with limited previous experience in data analysis develop the skills to use data effectively. Case study data across the five high schools suggest that the use of a data coach can reinforce a data-team structure and help team members problem solve how to foster ongoing data use by school personnel whose time and energy is consumed by the daily demands and requirements of high school restructuring. Specific dimensions of the data coach role include: (a) procedural assistance in identifying and addressing data-quality issues and improving the use of data for schoolwide planning and improvement; and (b) modeling and skill-building assistance in focusing data use around critical questions, using data to monitor the progress of students on multiple measures, and identifying areas of strength in student learning as well as areas for intervention and additional support to students. The work of the data coach and the evolution of a data team structure varied somewhat in the different high school sites based on the unique context of the school. However, the case study evidence indicates that as data teams mature, the role of a data coach decreases as team members and other school staff develop deeper understandings of the institutional function of data use in a school.

THE POLICY AND PRACTICE IMPLICATIONS OF IMPLEMENTING A DATA-USE PROCESS IN URBAN HIGH SCHOOLS

For high school leaders seeking to establish a schoolwide process of data use, the case study holds many lessons about factors that contribute to success. Not all of the high schools were equally successful in the progress they made over the 4-year period in establishing and sustaining effective data use by multiple school staff. However, they all made some progress, and they were all strongly committed to a continuous process of data use by the end of the study. An important aspect of this commitment was the fact that the use of data for continuous improvement was viewed as a central element, versus just an activity, in all of their reform plans. The lesson is that school leaders need to view and champion data use as integral to school reform processes.

Another important lesson is that many urban schools and districts would profit from a technical review of their procedures for collecting and updating student data. Districts may need stronger data-verification and data-management procedures to ensure the accurate and timely collection, storage, and analysis of essential data. The study also confirms research that cites the importance of data-warehousing technology in providing high-level data disaggregation and the capability to integrate or link multiple types of student performance data, demographic data, and data on students' educational experiences (Wayman et al., 2004). In an education reform context that requires the use of high-quality disaggregated data for the purposes of accountability and improvement, district leaders need to develop better understandings of this technology.

As highlighted in previous literature (Lachat, 2002; NFIE, 2003), the case study also shows that effective data use requires procedures for providing timely data to school staff. In particular, as high schools make the transition to SLCs, teacher teams need pertinent information about the students assigned to an SLC. Data access policies that help high schools get timely information on the characteristics and past performance of incoming freshmen can have a positive impact on the school's ability to immediately provide interventions that reduce literacy achievement gaps. This is particularly important in high-poverty urban settings where many students enter high schools with poor literacy skills. The study also highlights the need for better communication between school personnel and the people who control data in a district. This is essential to ensuring the efficient transfer of data and to helping schools move beyond their role as "data providers" toward the role of "data users."

The case study also supports the importance of teacher collaboration in analyzing data around a set of clearly defined questions (Holcomb, 2001; Love, 2000). School leaders need to recognize, however, that the practice of collaborative inquiry requires sufficient time for staff to have data-driven conversations. Securing adequate, uninterrupted meeting time is essential to examining the implications of data and exploring options for improvement. Contract issues and the multiple demands on school staff during a high school restructuring process need to be recognized as potential barriers. School policies that integrate the use of data into staff meetings already occurring in the school, such as department meetings and SLC meetings, can overcome time barriers. For example, schools that have established common planning time for teacher teams can set an expectation that teachers will schedule time on a regular basis to examine a variety of student performance data.

The implementation of a schoolwide data-use process in low-performing high schools is greatly enhanced by leadership structures that mutually involve the principal and other administrators, teacher teams, department chairs, and a data team. The case study suggests that the multiple roles played by different school staff contribute to more widespread use of data. The efforts of data team members can be particularly important in increasing communication among school staff about trends and issues shown in the data. To increase their effectiveness, the data team should be representative of school leadership, teachers, SLC structures, and department structures. This can be accomplished by maintaining a relatively small data team with a nucleus of permanent members and including other personnel in targeted data use meetings and follow-up activities.

Finally, the study illustrates how the type of facilitation assistance provided by a data coach contributes to the use of data for accountability and improvement. A data coach can help build school staff capacity to use data by providing procedural assistance in addressing data-quality and data-access issues, as well as by modeling various uses of data by different school staff.

ACKNOWLEDGMENTS

This case study is being supported by funds from the Institute of Education Sciences, U. S. Department of Education.

REFERENCES

American Association of School Administrators. (2002). *Using data to improve schools: What's working*. Retrieved November 30, 2004, from http://www.aasa.org/cas/UsingDataToImproveSchools.pdf

Armstrong, J., & Anthes, K. (2001). How data can help: Putting information to work to raise student achievement. *American School Board Journal, 188*(11), 38–41.

Bernhardt, V. L. (1998). *The school portfolio: A comprehensive framework for school improvement* (2nd ed.). Larchmont, NY: Eye on Education.

Bernhardt, V. L. (2000a). *Databases can help teachers with standards implementation*. Retrieved November 30, 2004, from http://www.educationadvisor.info/documents/OCIO2001/DatabasesCanHelp.pdf

Bernhardt, V. L. (2000b). Intersections. *Journal of Staff Development, 21*(1), 33–36.

Brimijoin, K., Marquissee, E., & Tomlinson, C. A. (2003). Using data to differentiate instruction. *Educational Leadership, 60*(5), 70–73.

Center for Collaborative Education. (2002, April). *The role of external facilitators in whole school reform: Teachers' perceptions of how coaches influence school change*. Paper presented at the annual meeting of the American Educational Research Association, New Orleans, LA.

Center for Collaborative Education. (2003). *The challenge of coaching: Providing cohesion among multiple reform agendas*. Boston: Author. Retrieved November 30, 2004, from http://www.ccebos.org/coaching_challenge.2004.pdf

Chrispeels, J. H. (1992). *Purposeful restructuring: Creating a climate of learning and achievement in elementary schools*. London: Falmer.

Cizek, G. J. (2000). Pockets of resistance in the assessment revolution. *Educational Measurement: Issues and Practice, 19*(2), 16–33.

Codding, J. B., & Rothman, R. (1999). Just passing through: The life of an American high school. In D. D. Marsh & J. B. Codding (Eds.), *The new American high school* (pp. 3–17). Thousand Oaks, CA: Corwin.

Cromey, A. (2000). Using student assessment data: What can we learn from schools? *Policy Issues, 6*. Retrieved November 30, 2004, from the North Central Regional Educational Laboratory Web site: http://www.ncrel.org/policy/pubs/html/pivol6/nov2000.htm

Earl, L., & Katz, S. (2002). Leading schools in a data-rich world. In K. Leithwood & P. Hallinger (Eds.), *Second international handbook of educational leadership and administration* (pp. 1003–1024). Dordrecht, Netherlands: Kluwer.

Feldman, J., & Tung, R. (2001). Using data-based inquiry and decision making to improve instruction. *ERS Spectrum, 19*(3), 10–19.

Greene, T. (2004, July). *Literature review for school-based staff developers and coaches.* Oxford, OH: National School Development Council. Retrieved April 29, 2005 from http://www.nsdc.org/library/schoolbasedlitreview.pdf

Holcomb, E. L. (1999). *Getting excited about data: How to combine people, passion, and proof.* Thousand Oaks, CA: Corwin.

Holcomb, E. L. (2001). *Asking the right questions: Techniques for collaboration and school change* (2nd ed). Thousand Oaks, CA: Corwin.

Johnson, R. (1996). *Setting our sights: Measuring equity in school change.* Los Angeles: The Achievement Council.

Johnson, R. (2002). Using data to close the achievement gap: How to measure equity in our schools (1st ed.). Thousand Oaks, CA: Corwin.

Keeney, L. (1998, May). Using data for school improvement. In *Tools for Accountability Project, Report on the Second Practitioners' Conference for Annenberg Challenge Sites, Houston, TX.* Retrieved November 30, 2004, from Brown University, Annenberg Institute for School Reform Web site: http:www.annenberginstitute.org/images/using_data4.pdf

Kennedy, E. (2003). *Raising test scores for all students: An administrator's guide to improving standardized test performance.* Thousand Oaks, CA: Corwin.

Killion, J., & Bellamy, G. T. (2000). On the job: Data analysts focus school improvement efforts. *Journal of Staff Development, 21*(1), 27–31.

Lachat, M. (2002). *Data-driven high school reform: The breaking ranks model.* Providence, RI: Brown University, Northeast and Islands Regional Educational Laboratory.

Lachat, M., & Williams, M. (2003). Putting student performance data at the center of school reform. In J. DiMartino, J. Clark, & D. Wolk (Eds.), *Personalized learning* (pp. 210–228). Lanham, MD: Scarecrow.

Love, N. (2000). *Using data, getting results: Collaborative inquiry for school-based mathematics and science reform.* Cambridge, MA: Regional Alliance at TERC.

Marzano, R. J. (2003). Using data: Two wrongs and a right. *Educational Leadership, 60*(5), 56–60.

Mason, S. (2002, April). *Turning data into knowledge: Lessons from six Milwaukee public schools* (WCER Working Paper No. 2002-3). Retrieved November 30, 2004, from University of Wisconsin, School of Education, Wisconsin Center for Education Research Web site: http://www.wcer.wisc.edu/publications/workingpaper/paper/Working_Paper_No_2002_3.pdf

National Education Association Foundation for the Improvement of Education. (2003). *Using data about classroom practice and student work to improve professional development for educators.* Retrieved November 30, 2004, from http://www.nfie.org/publications/usingdataIB.pdf

North Central Regional Educational Laboratory. (2003). Painting by number: Using data to create a portrait of school improvement. In *NCREL's Learning Point.* Retrieved November 30, 2004, from http://www.ncrel.org/info/nlp/lpf03/paint.htm

Olson, L. (2002, June 12). Schools discovering riches in data. *Education Week on the Web.* Retrieved November 30, 2004, from http://www.edweek.org/ew/articles/2002/06/12/40data.h21.html?querystring=schools%20discovering%20riches%20in%20data%202002

Pardini, P. (2000). Data, well done: Six examples of data-driven decision making at work. *Journal of Staff Development, 21*(1), 12–18.

Protheroe, N. (2001). Improving teaching and learning with data-based decisions: Asking the right questions and acting on the answers. *Educational Research Service Spectrum, 19*(3). Retrieved November 30, 2004, from http://www.ers.org/spectrum/sum01a.htm

Rallis, S. F., & MacMullen, M. M. (2000). Inquiry-minded schools: Opening doors for accountability. *Phi Delta Kappan, 81,* 766–773.

RAND Corporation. (2002). *A decade of whole-school reform: The New American Schools experience.* Santa Monica, CA: Author.

Rudner, L. M., & Boston, C. (2003). Data warehousing: Beyond disaggregation. *Educational Leadership, 60*(5), 62–65.

Schmoker, M. (2003). First things first: Demystifying data analysis. *Educational Leadership, 60*(5), 22–24.

Schwartz, W. (2002). Data-driven equity in urban schools. (ERIC Digest). Retrieved November 30, 2004, from http://www.ericdigests.org/2003-2/data.html

Streifer, P. A. (2002, July). *Data-driven decision-making: What is knowable for school improvement.* Paper presented at the National Center on Education Statistics (NCES) Summer Data Conference, Washington, DC. Retrieved November 30, 2004, from http://www.edsmartinc.com/whitepapers/what_is_knowable.doc

Thorn, C. A. (2001). Knowledge management for educational information systems: What is the state of the field? *Educational Policy Analysis Archives, 9*(47), 1–31. Retrieved November 30, 2004, from http://epaa.asu.edu/epaa/v9n47/

Visher, M. G., & Hudis, P. M. (1999). *Aiming high: Strategies to promote high standards in high schools* [Interim report]. Washington, DC: U.S. Department of Education, Office of Vocational and Adult Education.

Wade, H. H. (2001). Data inquiry and analysis for educational reform. (ERIC Digest). Retrieved November 30, 2004, from http://www.ericdigests.org/2002-4/data-inquiry.html

Wayman, J. C., & Stringfield, S. (2003, October). *Teacher-friendly options to improve teaching through student data analysis.* Paper presented at the 10th annual meeting of the American Association for Teaching and Curriculum, Baltimore. Retrieved November 30, 2004, from http://www.csos.jhu.edu/systemics/datause/papers/AATC_Teacher-Friendly_Software.pdf

Wayman, J. C., Stringfield, S., & Yakimowski, M. (2004). *Software enabling school improvement through analysis of student data* (Report No. 67). Baltimore: Johns Hopkins University, Center for Research on the Education of Students Placed At Risk.

NOTES ON CONTRIBUTORS

KATHRYN PARKER BOUDETT is a lecturer at the Harvard Graduate School of Education (HGSE). She is the current teacher of the course for HGSE students and Boston public school educators about how to make constructive use of student assessment results.

CORNELIA BRUNNER, associate director of the Center for Children and Technology (CCT), has been involved in the research, production, and teaching of educational technology in a variety of subject areas for 30 years. In addition to extensive research experience, Dr. Brunner has designed and implemented educational materials incorporating technologies to support inquiry-based learning and teaching in science, social studies, media literacy, and the arts.

EVA CHEN is a senior researcher at the National Center for Research on Evaluation, Standards and Student Testing (CRESST) at the University of California, Los Angeles. Dr. Chen's research interests center on computer integration in educational settings. Her research also examines how parents supplement home schooling with resources on the computer.

MARGARET HERITAGE is the assistant director for professional development at CRESST at the University of California, Los Angeles. Dr. Heritage has participated in a wide variety of research initiatives and published on topics including literacy, children's personal and social development, curriculum development, and school management. She is involved in the Quality School Portfolio (QSP) initiative to help schools engaged in local reform efforts develop their capacity to use and report on student information.

MARY ANN LACHAT is the president of the Center for Resource Management, Inc., where she has conducted extensive research on uses of database technology to support education reform, as well as the core capacities essential to data-driven decision making.

JOHN LEE is a senior researcher at CRESST. His current research is dedicated to working on the QSP project, with a particular focus on software development. He also coordinates the Los Angeles schools involved in the QSP Training Initiative funded by the Stuart Foundation. His research interests include data-informed decision-making processes.

CHAD FASCA serves as staff editor for CCT.

JULIETTE HEINZE, a research associate at CCT, has extensive experience in teaching and program organization, both domestically and internationally.

MARGARET HONEY, director of CCT and vice president of the Education Development Center (EDC), has worked in the field of educational technology since 1981. Dr. Honey's primary research interests include the role of technology in school reform and student achievement, the use of telecommunications technology to support online learning communities, and issues of equity associated with the development and use of technology.

DANIEL LIGHT, a senior researcher at CCT, has a background in qualitative and quantitative sociological research methodologies. Dr. Light's research interests include the social issues of school reform and technology integration across school systems.

ELLEN MANDINACH, associate director for research at CCT, has done extensive work in the field of educational technology. She has a strong background in research methodologies. Dr. Mandinach's research has focused on the implementation and impact of computer environments on learning and the measurement of individual differences in cognitive and affective processes.

RICHARD J. MURNANE, an economist, is Thompson Professor of Education and Society at the HGSE. His most recent book (with Massachusetts Institute of Technology Professor Frank Levy) is titled *The New Division of Labor: How Computers Are Creating the Next Job Market*.

JEFFREY SCHUMANN has been a professional educator for 26 years. He will be completing a PhD in Educational Leadership at the University of Connecticut in the spring of 2005.

NANCY S. SHARKEY is an advanced doctoral student at the HGSE. Her research explores how and why teachers use student assessment results to inform instruction and the district role in that process.

STEPHEN SMITH is a senior associate at the Center for Resource Management, Inc., where he coordinates technical assistance services that focus on strategic uses of data at district and school levels.

PHILIP STREIFER is an associate professor at the University of Connecticut and the founder of EDsmart Inc., a subsidiary of Public Consulting Group, Boston, MA. Dr. Streifer is a former superintendent of schools in Connecticut and Rhode Island.

JEFFREY C. WAYMAN is an associate research scientist with the Center for Social Organization of Schools at Johns Hopkins University. His research interests include educational data use, educator support and preparation, and school dropout issues.

DARA WEXLER is a research associate at CCT. Dr. Wexler has primary research interests in the study of popular cultural representations, the process of technology integration, building collaborative communities, media and digital literacy, and exploring power relationships between educators and learners.

PSYCHOPATHOLOGY
Foundations for a Contemporary Understanding

Edited by
JAMES E. MADDUX
George Mason University
BARBARA A. WINSTEAD
Old Dominion University

Psychopathology: Foundations for a Contemporary Understanding is specifically designed to meet the needs of *graduate students* enrolled in a one semester course on abnormal psychology or psychopathology in master's or doctoral programs in clinical and counseling psychology and related fields, such as social work. Neither an undergraduate abnormal text (though suitable for use in advanced courses that presuppose a basic abnormal course) nor a handbook-style compendium for professionals and researchers, it synthesizes the latest knowledge about the etiology and treatment of the most important psychological disorders, and challenges students to reflect on such crucial and controversial issues as the definition of psychopathology, the influence of culture and gender, the validity of psychological testing, and the viability and utility of traditional psychiatric diagnosis.

The authors, all leading experts, focus throughout on what has been demonstrated by *research*, not on what has been claimed by theories that may be accepted or traditional but lack empirical support. The first section presents and analyzes the basic concepts we need to understand any disorder; the second examines the disorders most frequently encountered in clinical practice.

The editors have brought to their job a combined total of 47 years of teaching graduate students.

Well-organized and clearly written, *Psychopathology: Foundations for a Contemporary Understanding* is an invaluable new resource for instructors and students alike.

Contents: Preface. Part I: *Thinking About Psychopathology.* J.E. Maddux, J.T. Gosselin, B.A. Winstead, Conceptions of Psychopathology: A Social Constructionist Perspective. S.R. L'opez, P.J. Guarnaccia, Cultural Dimensions of Psychopathology: The Social World's Impact on Mental Illness. B.A. Winstead, J. Sanchez, Gender and Psychopathology. T.A. Widiger, Classification and Diagnosis: Historical Development and Contemporary Issues. H.N. Garb, S.O. Lilienfeld, K.A. Fowler, Psychological Assessment and Clinical Judgment. R.H. Howland, Biological Bases of Psychopathology. Part II: *Common Adult, Adolescent, and Child Disorders.* S.L. Williams, Anxiety Disorders. R. Ingram, L. Trenary, Mood Disorders. E. Walker, A. Bollini, K. Hochman, L. Kestler, Schizophrenia. L.A. Coker, T.A. Widiger, Personality Disorders. J. Polivy, C.P. Herman, M. Boivin, Eating Disorders. N. McConaghy, Sexual Dysfunctions and Disorders. G.H. Eifert, M.J. Zvolensky, Somatoform Disorders. W. Fals-Stewart, Substance Use Disorders. P.J. Frick, E.R. Kimonis, Externalizing Disorders of Childhood and Adolescence. T.H. Ollendick, A.L. Shortt, J.B. Sander, Internalizing Disorders of Childhood and Adolescence. J. Naglieri, C. Salter, J. Rojahn, Cognitive Disorders of Childhood and Adolescence: Specific Learning Disabilities and Mental Retardation. K.H. Sorocco, L.M. Kinoshita, D. Gallagher-Thompson, Mental Health and Aging: Current Trends and Future Directions.
0-8058-4077-X [cloth] / 2005 / 480pp. / $55.00
Prices are subject to change without notice.

LAWRENCE ERLBAUM ASSOCIATES
www.erlbaum.com

Toll-Free: 1-800-926-6579 ◇ E-mail: orders@erlbaum.com ◇ Fax: 201-760-3735

2005 SUBSCRIPTION ORDER FORM

JOURNAL OF EDUCATION FOR STUDENTS PLACED AT RISK
Volume 10, 2005, Quarterly — ISSN 1082-4669/Online 1532-7671

SUBSCRIPTION PRICES PER VOLUME:

Please ❑ enter ❑ renew my subscription:

Category:	Access Type:	Price: (U.S.-Canada/All Other Countries)
❑ Individual	Online & Print	$50.00/$80.00

Subscriptions are entered on a calendar-year basis only and must be paid in advance in U.S. currency—check, credit card, or money order. Prices for subscriptions include postage and handling. **Journal prices expire 12/31/05. NOTE:** Institutions must pay institutional rates. Individual subscription orders are welcome if prepaid by credit card or personal check. **Please note:** A $20.00 penalty will be charged against customers providing checks that must be returned for payment. This assessment will be made only in instances when problems in collecting funds are directly attributable to customer error.

❑ Check Enclosed (U.S. Currency Only)   Total Amount Enclosed $ _____

❑ Charge My: ❑ VISA   ❑ MasterCard   ❑ AMEX   ❑ Discover

Card Number _____ Exp. Date ____ / ____

Signature _____
(Credit card orders cannot be processed without your signature.)
PRINT CLEARLY for proper delivery. STREET ADDRESS/SUITE/ROOM # REQUIRED FOR DELIVERY.

Name _____

Address _____

City/State/ Zip+4 _____

Daytime Phone # _____ E-mail address _____

Prices are subject to change without notice. Direct all inquiries and orders to the address below.
For information about online journal access, visit our web site at: www.LEAonline.com

LIBRARY RECOMMENDATION FORM

JOURNAL OF EDUCATION FOR STUDENTS PLACED AT RISK
Volume 10, 2005, Quarterly — ISSN 1082-4669/Online 1532-7671

Category:	Access Type:	Price: (U.S.-Canada/All Other Countries)
❑ Institutional	Online & Print	$395.00/$425.00
❑ Institutional	Online Only	$355.00/$355.00
❑ Institutional	Print Only	$375.00/$405.00

Name _____ Title _____

Institution /Department _____

Delivery Address _____

E-Mial Address _____
Complete and forward to your librarian. Librarians, please send your orders directly to LEA or contact your subscription agent.

DIRECT ALL SUBSCRIPTION ORDERS TO:
Lawrence Erlbaum Associates, Inc.,
Journal Subscription Department; 10 Industrial Avenue, Mahwah, NJ 07430
(201) 258–2200; FAX (201) 760–3735; journals@erlbaum.com

LEA LAWRENCE ERLBAUM ASSOCIATES

LEA *Online*
WWW.LEAONLINE.COM

INTERVIEWING AND DIAGNOSTIC EXERCISES FOR CLINICAL AND COUNSELING SKILLS BUILDING

PEARL S. BERMAN, *Indiana University of Pennsylvania*
With
SUSAN N. SHOPLAND

Advance praise... *"Through rich and compelling case profiles, Berman and Shopland's unique text is likely to fully engage the fledgling clinician in the process of acquiring essential interviewing skills. Classroom use of the thought-provoking exercises they've devised is likely to invigorate class atmosphere, making it an effective workplace for skill mastery. This text is unlike others in that diversity is not an afterthought; it requires students to take into account the differences among individuals at the beginning of the diagnostic enterprise."*
—Virginia Brabender, Ph.D.
Institute for Graduate Clinical Psychology, Widener University

This book, specifically designed to meet the needs of those teaching and learning interviewing and diagnostic skills in clinical, counseling and school psychology, counselor education, and other programs preparing mental health professionals, offers a rich array of practical, hands-on, class- and workshop-tested role-playing and didactic exercises.

The authors, who bring to their task a combined 31 years of practice and 24 years of teaching these skills, present 20 complex profiles of a broad range of clients—adults, teens, and children; differing in ethnicity, gender, religion, socioeconomic status, presenting problems, and problem severity. The profiles provide students/trainees with a wealth of information about each client's feelings, thoughts, actions, and relationship patterns on which to draw as they proceed through the different phases of the intake/initial interview, one playing the client and one the interviewer. Each client profile is followed by exercises, which can also be assigned to students not participating in role-playing who have simply read the profile.

The profiles are detailed enough to support a focus on whatever interviewing skills an instructor particularly values. However, the exercises highlight attending, asking open and closed questions, engaging in reflective listening, responding to nonverbal behavior, making empathetic comments, summarizing, redirecting, supportively confronting, and commenting on process. The authors' approach to DSM-IV diagnoses encourages students to develop their diagnostic choices from Axis I to Axis V and then thoughtfully review them in reverse order from Axis V to Axis I to ensure that the impacts of individual, situational, and biological factors are all accurately reflected in the final diagnoses. Throughout, the authors emphasize the importance of understanding diversity and respecting the client's perceptions—and of reflecting on the ways in which the interviewer's own identity influences both the process of interviewing and that of diagnosis.

Interviewing and Diagnostic Exercises for Clinical and Counseling Skills Building will be welcomed as a invaluable new resource by instructors, students, and trainees alike.
0-8058-4640-9 [paper] / 2005 / 312pp. / $42.50

Complete table of contents are available online at:
www.erlbaum.com

LAWRENCE ERLBAUM ASSOCIATES
www.erlbaum.com

Toll-Free: 1-800-926-6579 ◊ E-mail: orders@erlbaum.com ◊ Fax: 201-760-3735

CONTROVERSIAL THERAPIES FOR DEVELOPMENTAL DISABILITIES
Fads, Fashion, and Science in Professional Practice

Edited by
JOHN W. JACOBSON
Sage Colleges Center for Applied Behavior Analysis
RICHARD M. FOXX
Pennsylvania State University, Harrisburg
JAMES A. MULICK
Ohio State University

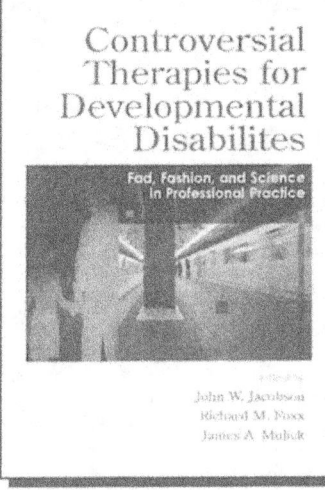

One of the largest and most complex human services systems in Western nations has evolved to address the needs of people with developmental disabilities. In the U.S., for example, school budgets are stretched thin by legally mandated special education, and billions of Medicaid dollars annually are consumed by residential and professional services to this population.

The temptation of a quick fix is strong. Many parents desperately seek the latest ideas and place pressure on program administrators, who often are not trained to think critically about the evidence base for intervention efforts. The problems of people with developmental disabilities have historically been targeted by a wide range of professionals who rely on clinical experience and intuition and do not submit their claims to the tests of scientific research. Professional entrepreneurs have energetically promoted their treatments to a public perhaps too trustful of those with credentials.

Thus, families and their children are buffeted by reforms founded on belief and ideologically driven management. Services fluctuate with the currents of social movements and rapidly shifting philosophies of care as policymakers and providers strive for increased responsiveness and individualization. These forces affect not only where and how, but how well people are served. Too often, services are less effective than they could be, or worse, damaging to personal growth and quality of life. Many treatments are based on poorly understood or even disproven approaches.

What approaches to early intervention, education, therapy, and remediation really help those with mental retardation and developmental disabilities improve their functioning and adaptation? And what approaches represent wastes of time, effort, and resources?

This book brings together leading behavioral scientists and practitioners to focus light on the major controversies surrounding these questions. The authors review the origins, perpetuation, and resistance to scrutiny of questionable practices, and offer a clear rationale for appraising the quality of services.

In an era of increasing accountability, no one with a professional stake in services to individuals with mental retardation and developmental disabilities can afford not to read this book.

0-8058-4191-1 [cloth] / 2005 / 528pp. / $125.00
0-8058-4192-X [paper] / 2005 / 528pp. / $49.95
Prices are subject to change without notice.

Complete Table of Contents and expert testimonials are available online at:
www.erlbaum.com

LAWRENCE ERLBAUM ASSOCIATES
www.erlbaum.com

Toll-Free: 1-800-926-6579 ◊ E-mail: orders@erlbaum.com ◊ Fax: 201-760-3735

SCHOOLS OR MARKETS?
Commercialism, Privatization, and School-Business Partnerships

Edited by
DERON R. BOYLES, *Georgia State University*

"I'm impressed by the seriousness of the scholarship as well as the number of issues this book raises in relation to its topic, including globalization, democracy, and the changing nature of knowledge. For any scholar interested in privatization of education, school commercialism, or contemporary sociology of education this is an essential book to read."

—Kenneth Saltman
Depaul University

This book challenges readers to consider the consequences of commercialism and business influences on and in schools. Critical essays examine the central theme of commercialism via a unique multiplicity of real-world examples. Topics include: privatization of school food services; oil company ads that act as educational policy statements; a parent's view of his child's experiences in a school that encourages school-business partnerships; commercialization and school administration; teacher union involvement in the school-business partnership craze currently sweeping the nation; links between education policy and the military-industrial complex; commercialism in higher education, including marketing to high school students, intellectual property rights of professors and students, and the bind in which professional proprietary schools find themselves; and the influence of conservative think tanks on information citizens receive, especially concerning educational issues and policy.

Schools or Markets? Commercialism, Privatization, and School-Business Partnerships is compelling reading for all researchers, faculty, students, and education professionals interested in the connections between public schools and private interests. The breadth and variety of topics addressed make it a uniquely relevant text for courses in social and cultural foundations of education, sociology of education, educational politics and policy, economics of education, philosophy of education, introduction to education, and cultural studies in education.

Contents: A. Molnar, Foreword. Preface. C. VanderSchee, The Privatization of Food Services in Schools: Undermining Children's Health, Social Equity, and Democratic Education. L. Trammell, Measuring and Fixing, Filling and Drilling: The ExxonMobile Agenda for Education. R. Hewitt, Priming the Pump: "Educating" for Market Democracy. D.A. Breault, Jesus in the Temple: What Should Administrators Do When the Marketplace Comes to School? B. Weiss, Teachers, Unions, and Commercialization. J. Block, Children as Collateral Damage: The Innocents of Education's War for Reform. B. Baez, Private Knowledge, Public Domain: The Politics of Intellectual Property in Higher Education. G.A. Miller, The Two-Way Street of Higher Education Commodification. L. Stultz, Egocentrism in Professional Arts Education: Toward a Discipline-Based View of Work and World. L. Wilson, Controlling the Power Over Knowledge: Selling the Crisis for Self-Serving Gains. D. Boyles, The Exploiting Business: School Business Partnerships, Commercialization, and Students as Critically Transitive Citizens.
0-8058-5203-4 [cloth] / 2005 / 272pp. / $79.95
0-8058-5204-2 [paper] / 2005 / 272pp. / $32.50
Prices are subject to change without notice.

LAWRENCE ERLBAUM ASSOCIATES
www.erlbaum.com

Toll-Free: 1-800-926-6579 ◊ E-mail: orders@erlbaum.com ◊ Fax: 201-760-3735

ORGANIZED ACTIVITIES AS CONTEXTS OF DEVELOPMENT

Extracurricular Activities, After School and Community Programs

Edited by

JOSEPH L. MAHONEY, *Yale University*
REED W. LARSON, *University of Illinois at Urbana-Champaign*
JACQUELYNNE S. ECCLES, *University of Michigan-Ann Arbor*

School-aged children in the U.S. and other Western nations spend almost half of their waking hours in leisure activities. How young persons can best use this discretionary time has been a source of controversy. For some, out-of-school time is perceived as inconsequential or even counterproductive to the health and well-being of young persons. Recently, however, there has been a growing recognition that—along with family, peers, and school—the organized activities in which some youth participate during these hours are important contexts of emotional, social, and civic development. They provide opportunities for young persons to learn and develop competencies that are largely neglected by schools. At the same time, communities and national governments are now channeling considerable resources into creating organized activities for young people's out-of-school time. This volume brings together a multidisciplinary, international group of experts to provide conceptual, empirical, and policy-relevant advances in research on children's and adolescent's participation in the developmental contexts represented by extracurricular activities, and after-school and community programs.

Organized Activities as Contexts of Development provides a handbook-like coverage of research in this new emerging field. It considers a broad developmental time-span from middle childhood through early adulthood, providing information on how motivation, participation, and developmental experiences change as youth get older. Bringing together diverse cultural, theoretical, and methodological perspectives, the book presents research on organized activities. The contents cover one of the most salient topics in child and adolescent research, education, and social policy, placing consistent emphasis on developmental aspects and implications of organized activity participation for young persons. As such, the volume is designed to have broad appeal. Representing contributors from several fields of study—psychology, criminal justice, leisure science, sociology, human development, education, prevention, and public policy—the book is designed to appeal to students and scholars in all these areas. Additionally, the volume discusses practice and policy issues in research on organized, out-of-school activities, and is written to be of interest to professionals who administer programs and develop policy on youth.

0-8058-4430-9 [cloth] / 2005 / 568pp. / $130.00
0-8058-4431-7 [paper] / 2005 / 568pp. / $55.00
Prices are subject to change without notice.

Complete table of contents are available online at:
www.erlbaum.com

LAWRENCE ERLBAUM ASSOCIATES
www.erlbaum.com

Toll-Free: 1-800-926-6579 ◇ E-mail: orders@erlbaum.com ◇ Fax: 201-760-3735

THE DEVELOPMENT AND TREATMENT OF GIRLHOOD AGGRESSION

Edited by
Debra J. Pepler
York University, Ontario, Canada
Kirsten C. Madsen
The Hospital for Sick Children, Toronto, Canada
Christopher D. Webster,
Kathryn S. Levene
Earlscourt Child and Family Centre, Toronto, Canada

After decades of neglect, researchers have begun to focus attention on the development and outcomes of girlhood aggression. This comprehensive volume provides an account of some of the pioneering research in the field. Its central aims are to highlight current understanding, identify key components for preventing and treating the complex array of problems experienced by aggressive girls, and raise new questions for future research.

The perspectives presented by the authors highlight the diverse factors that moderate the emergence of aggression while offering insight into how to target that aggression at various stages of development. The problem is presented as a continuum from normative forms of behavior to extreme and serious attacks. The importance of relationships—particularly family relationships—is a theme that permeates the entire volume. A growing body of research indicates that aggression in girls is a predictor of long-term psychological, social, academic, health, and intergenerational problems. The knowledge provided by the authors has a tremendous potential to inform practice with troubled girls, their families, and support systems.

Contents: K. Goldberg, Foreword. D.J. Pepler, K. Madsen, Introduction: Girlhood Aggression: Building Bridges Between Research and Treatment. *Part I: Girls' Aggression: Developmental Issues.* D.J. Pepler, W. Craig, Aggressive Girls on Troubled Trajectories: A Developmental Perspective. K. Keenan, M. Stouthamer-Loeber, R. Loeber, Developmental Approaches to Studying Conduct Problems in Girls. K. McKnight, M. Putallaz, Commentary: A Relationship Focus on Girls' Aggressiveness and Conduct Disorder. *Part II: Girls' Physical Aggression.* R.H. Baillargeon, R.E. Tremblay, J.D. Wilms, Gender Differences in the Prevalence of Physically Aggressive Behaviors in the Canadian Population of Two-and Three-Year-Old Children. S. Miller-Johnson, B.L. Moore, M.K. Underwood, J.D. Coie, African American Girls and Physical Aggression: Does Stability of Childhood Aggression Predict Later Negative Outcomes? L. Pulkkinen, Commentary: New Research Approaches to the Study of Aggression. *Part III: The Social Nature of Girls' Aggression.* H. Xie, B.D. Cairns, R.B. Cairns, The Development of Aggressive Behaviors Among Girls: Measurement Issues, Social Functions, and Differential Trajectories. S. Artz, To Die For: Violent Adolescent Girls' Search for Male Attention. P. Verlaan, Commentary: The Importance of Social Context and Relationships in Female Aggression. *Part IV: Aggressive Girls in Treatment.* K.S. Levene, K.C. Madsen, D.J. Pepler, Girls Growing Up Angry: A Qualitative Study. L.D. Leve, P. Chamberlain, Girls in the Juvenile Justice System: Risk Factors and Clinical Implications. W.M. Craig, Commentary: The Treatment of Aggressive Girls: Same but Different? *Part V: Aggressive Girls Grow Up.* M. Zoccolillo, D. Paquette, R. Tremblay, Maternal Conduct Disorder and the Risk for the Next Generation. D.M. Stack, L.A. Serbin, A.E. Schwartzman, J. Ledingham, Girls' Aggression Across the Life Course: Long-Term Outcomes and Intergenerational Risk. J. McCord, Commentary: Aggression Among Females.
0-8058-4039-7 [cloth] / 2005 / 336pp. / $69.95
Special Discount Price! $34.50
Applies if payment accompanies order or for course adoption orders of 5 or more copies.
No further discounts apply.
Prices are subject to change without notice.

LEA LAWRENCE ERLBAUM ASSOCIATES
www.erlbaum.com

Toll-Free: 1-800-926-6579 ◊ E-mail: orders@erlbaum.com ◊ Fax: 201-760-3735

For Product Safety Concerns and Information please contact our EU
representative GPSR@taylorandfrancis.com
Taylor & Francis Verlag GmbH, Kaufingerstraße 24, 80331 München, Germany

www.ingramcontent.com/pod-product-compliance
Lightning Source LLC
Chambersburg PA
CBHW051528230426
43668CB00012B/1782